How to Push a Perambulator

First published in Great Britain in 2007 by

PRION
an imprint of the
Carlton Publishing Group
20 Mortimer Street
London W1T 3JW

ISBN 978-1-85375-613-9

Typeset by E-Type, Liverpool
Printed and bound in Great Britain by Mackays

This is a humour title; the reader should not treat it as a genuine book of advice. Some instructions are dangerous and must not be followed, such as eating crushed woodlice or drinking arsenic solutions. Please consult the services of a physician before following any medical or dietary advice given in this book or taking any remedies suggested in this book. Neither the authors nor the publisher can accept responsibility for, or shall be liable for, any accident, injury, loss or damage (including any consequential loss) that a reader may suffer after using the ideas, information, procedures or advice offered in this book. Where relevant, every effort has been made to acknowledge correctly the source and / or copyright holder and Carlton Books Limited apologises for any unintentional errors or omissions that will be corrected in future editions of this book.

How to Push a Perambulator

50 Lessons in the Lost Art
of Being a Mother

ALISON RATTLE & ALLISON VALE

Contents

To Paul, without whose dedication to housework and endless cups of tea (eventually) this book could not have been written.

AR xx

For Claire and Chris — Mam a Tad or diwedd!
With special thanks to the multi-lingual Aunty Chris, Aunty Sue and Jeremy.

AV xx

'An ugly baby is a very nasty object
— and the prettiest is frightful'

Queen Victoria

Introduction

This volume has been crafted for the benefit of the emergent and inexpert mother of genteel persuasion. Some years of studious observation have convinced the authors that *modern* mothers, almost without exception, simply do not possess the requisite knowledge with which to produce and raise a child efficiently whilst maintaining an unruffled and dignified composure. This book is the means by which we would intend to rectify that miserable situation and furnish all with the advantage of our scholarship. We trust that many may profit from the wisdom laid down within and form early good habits, and that much good may thereby be effected.

The fondness which a mother feels for her offspring, being one of the strongest instincts of our nature, is often supposed to need no further refinement. How misguided is this presumption! We hope to furnish you with boundless maternal intelligence, and trust that our labours awaken within you a deeper interest in the correct training of the rising generation.

It is an unfortunate truth that a disproportionate amount of suffering has fallen to the lot of women. We hope the sound advice contained within this volume will relieve some of the burden. If but one woman should thereby become enlightened to the methods of ingenious motherhood, our bosoms will swell with pride! If but one son be cleansed of the sin of self-pollution and one daughter be made appreciative of the constraints of her corsets, we will have triumphed in our endeavours! If but one mother relieves the agonies of childbirth with mesmerism, or avoids being delivered of a monster, our years of toil against the chaos of bad mothering will not have been in vain!

Thus, the following pages have not been written from any desire for literary acclaim. In all we have undertaken herein, we have striven to be intelligible and useful; we have distanced ourselves from both artful jargon and scholarly citation, such as are often produced by lesser, bumptious and conceited authors, moved by nothing higher than vanity and the profound desire to show their own learning. We have rather fashioned our advice so that it is palatable for all mothers of taste and refinement.

It is our earnest prayer that you find our words worthy of your attention. Should this prove to be the case, we are not unwilling for it to be regurgitated for the benefit of others. We deliver it up as a *Foundling Child* is relinquished by its wretched mother, to be disposed of as you will. We shall only add by way of persuasion, to reassure those who may yet be dubious of our counsel, that we are Mothers and have already practised the advice herein with the most enviable success.

How to Relieve the Ailments of Pregnancy

'LEECHES APPLIED TO THE TROUBLED PART AND
ABLUTIONS WITH COLD WATER WILL ENABLE YOU TO
SIT COMFORTABLY ONCE MORE.'

When first a woman finds herself encumbered with child, she is innocent of the ills which may befall her. While she remains the sweet vessel of her husband's pleasure, she will find herself with swollen belly many times over, and it is as well she is armed with knowledge and useful receipts with which to become the guardian of her own comfort and relief in the years to follow.

To avoid the worst ailments of this all too frequent condition, it would be prudent of all those in ignorance to take note of the following advice:

❖ Take pains to avoid all unnecessary and violent exercise, such as fast walking, dancing and climbing stairs.
❖ Avoid all situations which may subject you to objectionable sights and seeming danger.

❖ Avoid the indulgence of an inordinate appetite.

❖ Shun over-heated rooms and exciting beverages.

❖ Desist from over-taxing the mind with study.

❖ Guard against all outbursts of passion.

It is for your well-being and comfort of mind, that we hereby endeavour to enlighten you with the best of medical treatments gleaned from physicians of the highest standing.

For Unceasing Vomiting

The morning sickness is a disagreeable condition so often attendant upon the pregnant state. It is an unfortunate complaint, most reluctant to be relieved by any number of remedies. The very best, however (which many ladies of our acquaintance have found most efficacious), we take the liberty of laying down before you.

Take 4 ounces of lettuce water, 2 ounces each of syrup of poppies and syrup of marsh-meadow root, 4 drops of Prussic acid and a scruple of gum Arabic. Combine to a mixture and take a spoonful every half hour.

Another mixture to calm the sickness is to be made by taking 20 drops of ammonia, 2 grains of oyster shells, 4 drachms of cinnamon water and an infusion of quassia. Take this as a drink at seven o'clock and twelve o'clock each day.

For Pain in the Head

Should a pain in the head or an unaccustomed drowsiness seek to trouble you, then it is advised that a fair few ounces of blood be taken from the arm. Leeches applied to the temple may prove most soothing and opening the bowels by means of rhubarb would prove most expedient.

Troublesome Itchings

If it should be that you are brought to the brink of madness by an itch which will not abate, then a lotion of sugar of lead combined with distilled water should be freely applied.

Incontinence of Bodily Fluids

This condition may only be fully relieved upon giving birth, but may be lessened by lying frequently in a horizontal position. A judiciously fastened large sponge will serve to alleviate much embarrassment.

Piles

Leeches applied to the troubled part, and ablutions with cold water, will enable you to sit comfortably once more.

Swelling of the Ankles

This complaint is invariably suffered towards the end of the day when your belly is at its heaviest. It may be relieved by scarifying the distended parts with a lancet. Cloths soaked in a hot decoction of chamomile may be applied directly after.

Cramp of the Leg

This most painful of disorders may be relieved by rubbing on a liniment comprised of a half ounce of laudanum and sulphuric ether and one ounce of tincture of camphor.

Inadequate Nipples

There are many ladies who are naturally deficient of nipple, or who have caused the deficiency themselves by the constant wearing, since childhood, of tight bodices. For one hoping to suckle their impending infant there is a simple and efficient plan which will serve to remedy this disorder. Wrap two or three times around the base of the nipple, a woollen thread, and pull moderately tightly to encourage the nipple to sufficient prominence.

ADAPTED IN PART FROM *A TREATISE ON THE DISEASES OF MARRIED FEMALES* BY JOHN C. PETERS, 1854, AND ADVICE GIVEN IN *THE HOUSEHOLD CYCLOPEDIA* BY HENRY HARTSHORNE, MD, 1881

How to Suffer and Survive the Exquisite Torture of Childbirth

'IF YOU ALREADY HAVE OFFSPRING, THESE MUST BE PROVIDED FOR AND YOUR HUSBAND REMINDED OF HIS OBLIGATION TO ENDEAVOUR TO NURTURE THEM SHOULD YOUR ETERNAL ABSENCE PROVE IMMINENT.'

Rare is the woman who faces her first trial of labour without a clear image of what is to come. Any woman, who has not already been subjected to that torturous rack of childbirth, will surely have been attendant upon the labours of a sister, cousin or friend. Many of the better sorts of ladies gather about them their nearest and dearest to support them through such times, and take their share in the fear. As a consequence, so many young wives thereafter face the period of confinement with great trepidation. Death is a common consequence of the trial every wife must undergo, and she cannot proceed in denial of this fact. But a true lady is a-feared not so much on account of her imminent struggle with death itself, so much as dying *unprepared*. For this reason, you must make your arrangements, both earthly and heavenly, prior to taking to the delivery chamber. Attend church and feel yourself thoroughly absolved from sin. Then see to it that your household affairs are fully in order. If you already have offspring, these must be provided for, and your husband reminded of his obligation to endeavour to nurture them should your eternal absence prove imminent.

Your selection of midwife is crucial: there are many who do great mischief that have been forced into the profession through want of bread alone! Most will have received little or no training. Often, overbearing and superstitious midwives can do much hurt. Let none proceed as midwife to your labour that is not first properly recommended.

Childbirth is naturally a painful process that a lady of breeding must endure with all the patience of a Christian martyr. That said, there are *preternatural* elements of the delivery, which can occasion a far greater suffering. It is on these elements that we will now focus our attentions.

How to Speed a Slow Labour

No one can long endure the racking asunder of her bones and sinews, nor bear the dreadful sufferings of her inward parts, nor listen long to the bellowing of her bowels, without soon descending into mania and death. When a woman has endured a tremendous travail, all must be done to help speed her along. She must first be bled plentifully. Next, an emollient clyster should be prepared as given out below, and should be inserted into her back passage with care.

Also beneficial in these cases is the recommended receipts of Dr Culpeper for a dissolved swallow nest, which he assures his midwives is most efficacious in speeding a protracted labour (we find this remedy most palatable when drunk in tincture form with linseed and raspberry tea). Certainly helpful is that the woman be required to sit over streams of warm water with wet cloths laid across her belly. Furthermore, it is often proved most effective for the birth passage itself to be encouraged with the rubbing in of a little fresh butter. If fatigue should overwhelm her, provide her with a generous draft of wine or other cordial.

An emollient clyster for the speeding of a slow labour:

Mix six ounces each of linseed tea and new milk.
Add fifty or sixty drops of laudanum.
Pour into the bowels as required.

Where labour persists in a protracted state despite all best efforts to speed it along, a man-midwife must be sought as a matter of urgency. Where not even the man-midwife can help throw out the baby, he will be forced to perform an embryotomy, in which he will slice the baby, disconnecting its head or its limbs from its trunk, in order to extract it *in pieces* from the birth passage, thus sparing the mother's life.

How to Treat Haemorrhagic Flooding

This is often a consequence of labour. The woman should be positioned with her head low and she should be kept cool. Soak cloths in equal parts of vinegar, water and red wine and apply these to the belly, haunches and thighs. Replace with freshly soaked cloths as soon as they dry.

How to Treat Milk Fever

Hard, red and inflamed breasts can most often be eased with the application of a red cabbage leaf or a poultice of bread and milk, softened with a little oil and butter. However, on the occasion of an extreme fever, with intolerably sore breasts, we recommend the following receipts:

For a sore breast:

> Frogspawn water, four ounces
> White wine and water, of each, six ounces
> Crabs eyes, two drams
> Of sugar of lead, half an ounce .
> Mix together and take a spoonful whenever you
>   please.

For the same:

> Take of woodlice prepared and salt of wormwood, of
>   each, two drams
> Powder of Avon, two spoonfuls
> Mix and take a spoonful twice a day.

How to Suffer and Survive the Exquisite Torture of Childbirth

⸻

INSPIRED BY THE DIARIES OF ALICE THORNTON, WRITTEN IN THE 1630S, AND ADAPTED IN PART FROM ORIGINAL ADVICE IN CULPEPER'S *DIRECTORY FOR MIDWIVES*, D. PETRE'S *MEDICINAL COOKBOOK*, 1705, AND WILLIAM BUCHAN'S *DOMESTIC MEDICINE*, 1785

How to Relieve the Pains of
Labour with Mesmerism

'A GENTLEWOMAN'S VERY NATURE, BEING GOVERNED BY HER
IMAGINATION AND BEING NATURALLY OPEN AND SUBMISSIVE,
LENDS ITSELF MOST SUCCESSFULLY TO THE EFFECTS OF
MESMERISM. A WOMAN IS, AFTER ALL, BLESSED WITH THE
ABILITY TO RECEIVE INFORMATION WITHOUT QUESTIONING
THE AUTHORITY.'

I s it not true that, as descendants of Eve, all women of fertility are destined to suffer the agonies and sorrows of childbearing as punishment for the original sin? Indeed, is it not also said that the great waves of pain attendant upon labour are necessary to bring about the love and bonding of mother to child? Therefore, would it not be deemed blasphemous to be relieved of this torture by anything other than *natural* means?

It is as well then that we are able to instruct you to clasp your hands to your heaving bosoms and give thanks to the eminent Franz Anton Mesmer of Vienna who has introduced the marvels of mesmerism to the world and hence given all women of certain intellect the *natural* means by which to avoid the afflictions of procreation.

How to Relieve the Pains of Labour with Mesmerism

For what woman of gentility would wish to disgrace her demeanour by writhing and thrashing and howling like a wild animal during the final hours of her confinement? What lady of gentle sensibilities would willingly risk losing her composure and modesty upon the birthing bed? We have heard many tales of fine women who have suffered horrors beyond belief, their screams of torment unmuffled by closed doors. Many have lost their wits along with their eyesight and all feeling in the lower extremities whilst in the midst of a protracted and difficult labour. Surely none would welcome such abhorrence upon themselves?

For the price of a few pennies, one may attend a lecture in the effects of mesmerism (given by the many disciples of the genius Mesmer) and be dazzled by the strange power and influences of this extraordinary phenomenon. By bringing the natural forces of magnetism to bear on his subjects, the mesmerist is able to induce a state of sleep during which many cures may be effected. That mesmerism is part of the natural and spiritual order of things cannot be denied. Indeed, are not the forces of electricity or magnetism the very means by which God himself regulates Nature?

Many doubters would label the practice 'contemptible folly' and 'absurd humbug'.

But we have it on good authority that even that most respected of writers, the noble Charles Dickens, has been trained in the technique and has taken it upon himself to cure many friends and family members of their ailments. We have heard tell he rid the Madame de la Rue of her most debilitating nervous tic!

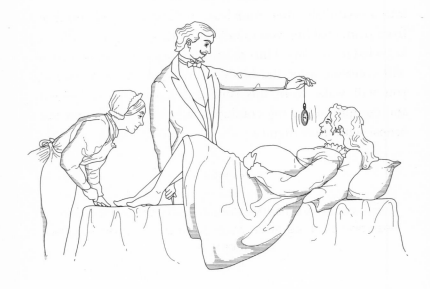

A gentlewoman's very nature, being governed by her imagination and being naturally open and submissive, lends itself most successfully to the effects of mesmerism. A woman is, after all, blessed with the ability to receive information without questioning the authority. It is therefore with great expectations that we recommend you secure for yourself during your pregnancy a prominent mesmerist, one who has filled halls and theatres through his reputation, and bid him come to your home the last week of your confinement. He will induce you into a mesmeric sleep by sitting himself in front of you with his knees resting upon your knees. He will press your thumbs into his hands and regard you fixedly in the eyes, occasionally passing his hands from your shoulders down your arms. You will experience a peculiar sensation, known as a *crisis*, before you slip into a restful slumber. Your body will be numbed and free from pain, enabling you to deliver a child *of any size* without knowledge or any hint of discomfort. The mesmerism will continue after the birth for your swift recovery and you will wake from this somnambulistic state refreshed and composed, having conducted yourself throughout the ordeal with utter dignity.

INSPIRED BY VICTORIAN ENGLAND'S FASCINATION WITH PSEUDO-SCIENCES SUCH AS PHRENOLOGY, SPIRITUALISM AND MESMERISM

How to Avoid the Delivery of Monstrous Babies and Rabbits

'WHATSOEVER SHOULD STARTLE A WOMAN WHEN SHE IS WITH CHILD, WILL BE THEREBY PASSED THROUGH TO HER UNBORN IN A MANNER MOST HORRIFYING.'

That a lady of refinement is an impressionable being, with a natural aversion toward anything of a fearful nature, cannot be questioned. From her earliest experiences, she is sheltered from all that is unseemly, that her sensibilities be not compromised. Never is it more essential to surround oneself with beauty, averting one's eyes from anything that might quicken the breath or raise the beat of the heart in shock, than when one is big with child. See that your treasures are carefully arranged, so that morning, noon and night you may cast your eyes upon works of breath-taking beauty. Have splendid floral arrangements made up daily. Banish plain and unsightly servants from parlour, boudoir and garden, lest you happen to meet their gaze directly. See that your lady's maid is of such innocent fair-face and your manservant of such strength and rugged beauty, that you may readily fix your eyes upon them at every opportunity. The more your eyes soak up the wondrous beauty of creation, the more you are likely to produce beauteous offspring.

Just as this last has been scientifically proven through the ages, so the corollary is alarmingly well-founded. The scientific theory of *Maternal Impressions* states it to be a fact that whatsoever should startle a woman when she is with child, will be thereby passed through to her unborn in a manner most horrifying. Many a woman upset by a violent din, or a hideous apparition, has been delivered of a monstrosity, the likes of which scarce bears retelling. We have heard a company of respected physicians tell of women who were wont to spend their restless pregnant hours gazing directly upon the moon and then bore children who became incurable sleep-walkers or, far worse, lunatics, due to the effect of that action upon the mind of their mother. And one eminent physician stunned all present company with an account of a woman startled and bitten by a rattle-snake in her seventh month. Two months on, she delivered a monster so hideous that it sent even the midwife quite lunatic: with the body shape and the teeth of a serpent, it never developed the ability to move in any other fashion than to slither along the ground like a venomous beast.

Much talked of some years ago was the case of a Parisian woman who was a misguided witness to the execution of a French ruffian upon the rack. The unborn child within her belly was thereafter *imprinted with the same traumas* as that wretched soul, and upon delivery was discovered to have the very same broken limbs as he.

Currently most infamous has been the case of Mary Toft of Godalming, who even under the direct care of the King's own physicians gave birth to numerous rabbits, all of whom died in the delivery. During her pregnancy she had been toiling in a field when a rabbit appeared and she developed a great longing for the flavour of it. She gave chase but to no avail. Thereafter, she was visited daily and nightly by such passionate desire for the flesh of rabbit that it seems the likeness was imprinted upon her unborn child. In total, and under the strictest scientific circumstances, the King's physician assured all at Court and the Royal Society of Surgeons that she had been delivered of seventeen rabbits or rabbit parts. All had perished inside her. We most heartily urge all

married ladies to desist from indulging in any ungratified longings when with child, lest a similar atrocity befall you.

To make certain that no evil can happen upon your child at the very last, within the delivery chamber itself, due care must be exercised here too. In addition to a well-respected midwife, it is vital that two God-fearing women are well chosen to act as your Godsips. They will seal the delivery room from evil, excluding all light from windows, sealing keyholes and cracks under the doors and ensure that no witchery is attempted by your midwife, as well as praying for you and your child throughout your labour. Moreover, they will keep you well informed with all that has occurred about the neighbourhood during your confinement.

Should you be blessed with a fully human baby, they will provide it with a temporary baptism, to safeguard it from evil until its church baptism can take place. In the unfortunate event that you are delivered of a monster (or, indeed, a rabbit), they will reserve a full bucket of water so that it may be instantly drowned for your own protection.

꧁꧂

INSPIRED BY THE CASE OF MARY TOFT OF GODALMING, WHO CONVINCED EMINENT SURGEONS THAT SHE HAD GIVEN BIRTH TO RABBITS IN SEPTEMBER 1726. SHE WAS CHARGED WITH BEING A 'VILE CHEAT AND IMPOSTER' BUT LATER DISCHARGED WITHOUT PROSECUTION

How to Survive a Man-Midwife

'A WOMAN OF MEANS MUST BE SEEN ABROAD TO PAY
GENEROUSLY FOR THE SERVICES OF A MAN-MIDWIFE OF
REPUTE IF SHE IS TO GIVE HER OFFSPRING THE VERY BEST
START IN LIFE.'

The labour and travail of a lady, as arduous as it is, must not be the occasion for letting drop those essential details that combine to convey that most coveted of public images: that of the socially adroit. Of all those minor points of form that assist in this respect, one currently most popular is that of securing the assistance of the very finest *man-midwife* during the labour of the elite. These gentlemen physicians offer the benefit of their significant learning, the like of which no ordinary midwife can hope to match.

That very fine physician, Dr William Smellie, a Scottish obstetrician of great renown, practised first his art upon an artificial doll, until he was certain of his craft. The science, mathematics and proven theories that combine to underpin the genius of such men is hard to rival! For such rare talent must the father-to-be expect to pay and dearly. Those whose talent is greatest are detectable by their greater fee. What ordinary midwife can be of equal substance, bereft as she is, of both any study of anatomy and of any keen presence of mind? All she can offer is the many hours she has spent practising her profession: for this her fee must necessarily remain meagre. No woman of substance can feel safe in the hands of one so lowly, so poorly rewarded financially, and one entirely lacking in any professional qualification save that she has delivered countless infants. A woman of means must be seen abroad to pay generously for the services of a man-midwife of repute if she is to give her offspring the very best start in life.

Those for whom pecuniary issues are of greater challenge, but whose social aspirations are nevertheless uppermost in their minds, could consider instead a self-professed man-midwife, as these still carry with them a certain cachet, but without commanding such a great fee. These men may not have received so extensive a training, but their backgrounds generally equip them to some degree for the task in hand. For example, barber-dentists, tailors and even butchers all have had occasion to develop some anatomical knowledge that can be turned to advantage in the labour room.

All this notwithstanding, it must be acknowledged that the success rate of the ordinary midwife is greater than any man-midwife to date. It is undeniable that many women deliver healthy, fully human babies, without any need for the intervention of the odious instruments, so fondly and commonly favoured by gentlemen physicians. A female midwife will, in ninety-five out of a hundred cases, deliver a woman of a baby without any cause to resort to butchery. Nevertheless, that constant eye one must devote to the maintenance of one's reputation and social standing dictates that a *man*-midwife it must be. With this in mind, we offer a few suggestions that will ensure that you deliver a healthy infant whilst not adversely affecting your own continued survival.

Firstly, make thorough enquiry in advance of your delivery as to the extent of your man-midwife's fondness of surgical tools. We ourselves have heard tell, from reliable sources, of infants born alive, but with *brains working outside of their skull*, because of the impatient use of such instruments by a man-midwife. Assure yourself in advance that such measures will only be undertaken in dire emergencies. Secondly, if thrift drives you to seek the assistance of a lesser, self-professed man-midwife, make thorough enquiry of his credentials, nevertheless. We know of one such individual, previously occupied in stuffing sausages, and yet now turned to the lucrative career of the delivery of babies, albeit with only dubious success.

There will always be some vicious opponents of the man-midwife. Such women as have previously made a living in this manner are certain to feel threatened by the new presence of the learned man in what has been her exclusive demesne to date. Gird yourself against the grim statistics of women butchered, maimed or killed at the hands of these individuals. Society expects that you *pay* for the finest, if you are to be seen as *party* to the finest. Seek the most costly as your purse will allow and make it known to all abroad that you have done so. Your children, should they survive, will thank you (or your memory) dearly in years to come.

INSPIRED BY THE DEBATE THAT RAGED IN EIGHTEENTH-CENTURY LITERATURE ABOUT THE MAN-MIDWIFE, AND IN PARTICULAR BY THE WRITINGS OF ELIZABETH NIHELL, PROFESSED MIDWIFE, IN *A TREATISE ON THE ART OF MIDWIFERY SETTING FORTH THE VARIOUS ABUSES THEREIN ESPECIALLY AS TO THE PRACTICE WITH INSTRUMENTS*, 1760

How to Swaddle a Baby

'SEE THAT THE CLOTHS ARE SOFT AND CLEAN, NOT TOO WORN OUT, AND THAT YOU DO NOT WRAP THEM SO TIGHT AS TO CRACK A RIB OR TURN THE INFANT'S FACE PUCE.'

A busy mother, distracted by the demands of her toilet and the excitements of society, will be loath to spend too great a portion of her day in watching over her newborn. The little creature is naught but a tender sapling with limbs flailing in all directions and a delicate constitution much given to injury and troubles. As a lady of respect and fragile sensibilities, your attentions are necessarily elsewhere, and an *unswaddled* child will prove a burden on your time and reputation. It is as well, then, to be well-tutored in the art of swaddling, for a well-wrapped child can be entrusted to a nursemaid or indeed to a corner of a room wherein its cries can be safely ignored.

As soon as your child has left the comfort of your womb, and before it has begun to move or stretch its limbs, see to it that the midwife wraps it tight in swathes, that it may at once be securely fastened.

The correct swaddling of a child may take some time to

perfect, but rest assured that once learned it will serve you well and may be completed in a matter of moments.

First, dress the infant in a front-opening linen shirt and make certain that its napkin is in position to catch any bodily emissions, which at such a tender age can be profuse. Lay the babe upon a cloth bed of wool flannel, the bottom of which should be turned up over his feet. Ensure that all parts to be bound are in their proper place with no crookedness, and lay the arms tight down by the sides, that they may grow straight. A quantity of linen swaddling bands, some three inches wide, should be wound spirally from the chest to the feet, then back again, trapping the arms inside. See that the cloths are soft and clean, not too worn out, and that you do not wrap them so tight as to crack a rib or turn the infant's face puce. Over the swaddling bands may be worn a waistcoat or robe, which we recommend to be of the finest silk and to extend many inches beyond the infant's length. Atop of this you may lay the burp cloth.

A swaddled infant rarely cries, its misshapen parts are duly corrected, its skin is rarely chafed, and no injury can befall its eyes from its own little fingers. In truth, a child thus swathed demands so little in the way of attention that one must take great pains in remembering to nourish it and remove its soiled napkins! The swaddling is of particular benefit to those infants born so feeble that a cough or a cry or a simple sneeze may rupture their delicate innards. The swathing affords a general support to the abdomen, hampering any tendency to injurious strains and assisting in correct digestion.

A child may be kept thus for the first year of its life, after which a loosening of its bands may be allowed for some freedom of the arms. The breast and feet should remain rolled, however, to keep out the cold air until the infant gains in strength.

Those mothers whose object it is to render a child's infancy a season of joy and comfort would not hesitate to confine one so — that it may grow straight and true and blossom forth like the strongest of oaks.

INSPIRED BY THE HISTORY OF SWADDLING
THROUGHOUT THE AGES

How to Organise a Christening

'YOUR GUESTS SHOULD BE ATTIRED MOST SPECTACULARLY;
THE LADIES BEDECKED WITH TIARAS AND JEWELS, AND
(SHOULD YOU BE SO FORTUNATE AS TO SECURE THEIR
PRESENCE) A CHOICE FEW UNIFORMED GENTLEMEN.'

None will deny the significance of the Christening of an infant. This most sacred of religious rituals marks a child's entry into the Church and all that is associated with that: weekly attendance, a deep and lasting faith and, the ultimate prayer, eternal life. It is only right and fitting, therefore, that such a momentous spiritual occasion is given over to the greatest pageantry, the grandest spectacle, the most pomp that your husband's coffers can permit! Indeed, all must know that no child will be given a finer start in life than yours. What better way to achieve this than to emulate the reverent Christenings of our own dear Royal family?

Commonly, a Christening takes place in the parish church and is but a brief affair, a mere half hour in duration and carried out in the presence of no more than a handful of the proud parents' nearest and dearest. The godparents are, no doubt, carefully selected; the babe presented in a clean white gown, and the ceremony followed in the afternoon by a light tea and the acceptance of a small few christening gifts; a silver spoon, cup or rattle usually fills the part.

Her Majesty Queen Victoria has seen fit to raise the status of the Christening to far loftier heights than this and all aspiring parents, especially where pecuniary constraints are few, would do well to follow suit.

If it is accepted that the white robe is symbolic of the purity of the baptised infant, then surely this robe should be substantial? No meagre measures will do. The finest Spitalfield satin was deemed fit for the Queen's first-born daughter, along with the most delicate lace (from Honiton in Devon, should one wish to follow Her Majesty's lead), laboured over for many hours by the hands of our nation's most highly skilled seamstresses. The royal lace took four hours to create each square inch: such dedication to the smallest detail is most commendable. Should you choose to follow suit, your utter devotion to every aspect of perfect motherhood will not go unnoticed.

Next, see to it that the Godparents are uncompromisingly respectable and utterly desirable, and that the guest list is both note-worthy and considerable. For the Christening of the future King in 1842, Queen Victoria spared no effort in gathering many to share this special day with her. So well attended was the ceremony that many guests later lamented that they could but steal the merest glimpse of the infant Prince of Wales from between the dressed heads, broad backs and bent elbows that pressed all around them. If your own occasion should succeed in raising similar complaints, how happy you will be, knowing you will have given your babe such a start!

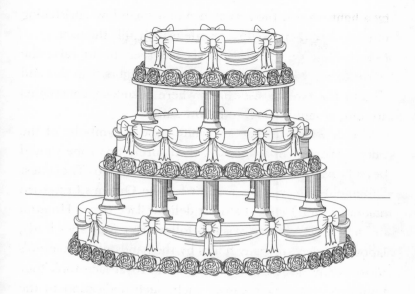

Your guests should be attired most spectacularly. What better way to ensure this than to time the Christening in the evening, so that guests will attend in all their finery, the ladies bedecked with tiaras and jewels, and (should you be so fortunate as to secure their presence) a choice few uniformed gentlemen, complete with decorations?

Finally, may we draw your attention to the Christening cake? Do not content yourself with some pitiful offering, decorated only with a simple posy or a few collaged scraps depicting cherubs, doves or garlands. How can this herald anything but a future of unstoppable mediocrity for your precious child? Again, we urge that you take a Royal lead in this matter. The Christening cake of the Prince of Wales formed the centrepiece of the banquet that followed, more so than the fireworks, or any other aspect of the *two hundred thousand pounds'* worth of trouble Her Majesty had taken over its organisation. The cake was of enormous dimensions, standing a magnificent four feet in height, and was reported by *The Times* to 'appear like a Coliseum of sugar'. Though the creators of this masterpiece are unattainable for any but royal households, you should make note of the ambitious nature of the confectionery when it comes to ordering your own design.

A Christening staged in such grandiose circumstances is certain to be greatly remarked upon for some time to follow.

⥌⥌

INSPIRED BY AN ARTICLE IN *THE TIMES*, 3 JUNE 1843, DESCRIBING THE CHRISTENING OF PRINCE ALBERT, THE INFANT PRINCE OF WALES, AND OTHER SOURCES ON QUEEN VICTORIA'S ELABORATE CHRISTENINGS

How to Push a Perambulator

'A CHILD IS LESS LIKELY TO TAKE A COLD WHEN BEING
PASSED BRISKLY THROUGH THE AIR IN A PERAMBULATOR,
NO MATTER HOW WARM AND WELCOMING SEEMS A NURSE'S
BOSOM!'

❧❧❧

E very devoted mother waits with barely concealed antici-
pation for the sweet days of spring to arrive. For it is
during this cleanest and freshest of seasons that the very
latest baby carriage catalogues arrive, whetting the appetite for the most stylish and sought-after of designs. You
may begin to imagine strolling once more in the dewy air,
contemplating all that Mother Nature has to offer, whilst
building up your health and constitution after an all too
long winter confined to the fusty parlour.

As a woman of privilege and good taste you will wish
to purchase the very best of perambulators, as befits your
place in society. It would be mere convenience, would
it not, that would bring you to place your order with
Hitchings Baby Stores of Ludgate Hill? Nothing more than
coincidence, that the self-same store provided Her Majesty
Queen Victoria with three of the most splendid of models
for the young Princes and Princesses!

How to Push a Perambulator

As Her Majesty found to her lasting delight, a perambulator fashioned from wicker provides all that is most desirable to be at one with Nature. With a lightweight and airy appearance, the wicker will afford the child a healthy amount of ventilation, whilst being most hygienic and easy to clean. Furthermore, its sturdy lightness will not tax the strength of any nursemaid when being manoeuvred from nursery to porch.

You may order your perambulator to be stained in a colour of your choosing, cherry, oak or mahogany being particularly pleasing. For mothers with the most exquisite of taste, gold leaf may be applied to the body of the perambulator to frame your travelling offspring in the richest of ways. Whilst the exterior of your chosen baby carriage will reflect your place in society, so too should the interior. The

softest of silks, the richest of damasks and the most intricate of tapestries should be used in the upholstery. Finally, the prettiest of parasols, trimmed with ruffles of lace, bows and luxuriant ribbons, should be hooked to the back of the carriage to complete the effect.

A well-chosen perambulator will display your family wealth and status in a most elegant manner.

It is the duty of your nursemaid to see to your child's ruddy good health, and it is she who will most often make use of the perambulator. If the weather be suitable, there is no cause why any child, from the very beginning, should not be wheeled out for its daily exercise. Indeed, most infants thrive in the open air. You must see to it that your nursemaid refrains from the despicable practice of carrying your child *in her arms*. Too many children are dropped on their heads when a nurse's arms become fatigued, and the streets are far too dirty to allow any young child to walk. She must make use of the perambulator at all times; it is only the lower classes, with no means to purchase a carriage, who persist in the risky and unhealthful business of transporting children by person. A child is less likely to take a cold when being passed *briskly* through the air in a perambulator, no matter how warm and welcoming seems a nurse's bosom!

All too often these days, one reads in *The Times* of members of the public who feel most inconvenienced by the novelty of sharing their space upon the pavements with a perambulator. Many would label these God-sent vehicles a nuisance and would complain of having their corns run over or, indeed, of being pushed off the pavement altogether!

Many, it would seem, would have the police interfere as if you were pushing a common truck of apples!

To avoid the very worst of these sore-heads, it would be best to push the perambulator around a public park with wide open spaces and sights of Nature on hand to entrance a little one. Instruct your nursemaid to always walk in a sedate manner, keeping hold of the perambulator handles at all times. She should not venture out in inclement weather and should avoid walking upon uneven ground, as a child may catch any number of fatal diseases when being wheeled about in such a manner. When stopping to rest, or to see to the needs of an accompanying child, a nurse must always be certain that the perambulator is resting on the flattest of ground. Alas, many a poor mother has grieved a child lost to the swiftness of a perambulator as it careered down a hill.

BASED ON THE HISTORY OF THE PERAMBULATOR, WHICH BECAME HUGELY POPULAR AMONG THE WEALTHY IN THE MID-1800S

How to Choose an Estimable Name

'TO SADDLE A GIRL WITH A NAME THAT IS WONT TO SINGLE
HER OUT, OR EVEN TO PLACE HER IN SOME DEGREE OF
LOCAL RENOWN, IS TO MAKE HER JOURNEY INTO DEMURE,
FEMININE OBSCURITY ALL THE HARDER.'

∞∽∾∾

There is assured status to be gained from a well-chosen Christian name. A lady with a regal, feminine title, or a gentleman with a firm, steadfast one, will go a good deal of the way towards creating the impression they seek, ever before he or she enters a room, simply upon the announcement of their name. *William Lucas,* or *Catherine de Bourgh,* command far more respect upon first hearing than does a more plebeian, *Molly Cooper,* for example. In this respect as in all others, a mother of ambitious persuasion would do well to adhere to those conventions that are widely respected in noble circles.

Our grandmothers were bound to pass on to their first born either the name of the paternal grandfather or the maternal grandmother. In time, it has (mercifully) become acceptable to pay our respects to our parents merely in the allocation of a *middle* name. Many will go further than simply choosing one middle name, and follow the royal lead in the allocation of a list of middle names, as a means of honouring respected and influential godparents, friends and other relatives. So long as the names selected are of a suitable propriety, this is a wholly acceptable convention: the Queen herself has six names, Alexandra Caroline Marie Charlotte Louise Julia.

But the trend of moving away from the confines of family names has resulted in a large degree of freedom to select all manner of first names for our children. Furthermore, it is an area in which many have fallen foul. Variation from convention is not a notion to be pandered to by any mother of genteel aspirations. Admittedly, there is a perceived allure in the allocation of names with strong literary or historical connotations. *Homer, Horatio, Edmund* and *Arthur* are impressive, in their own contexts, and will, in turn, impart a respectable and powerful impression. But consider the life-long woe that must follow if one is cursed by such parents as would, inspired by some mis-directed religious fervour, christen their sons *Fly-fornication, Kill-sin* or *Hate-evil*? A boy must be *blessed* by his name. It must ever stand him in good stead in society: what fortune can ever come to a man cursed with such an abhorrence for a name? Can one ever imagine a gentleman of title introducing himself as such? No? Precisely why it must be avoided at all costs.

Give your boy a name of substance: Joseph, William, John, James, Robert, Richard, Thomas, Henry or Charles. These names are most commonly taken up by respectable men across our land. If they have been deemed fitting for the offspring of these families, then surely they can be deemed appropriate for your sons, too?

The christening of our daughters is another area of concern. Here, too, one must proceed with caution. Regal or biblical names are all very well: Sarah, Mary, Elizabeth, Ann, are all much to be admired and have served generations of genteel women well. Lately, a leaning towards Christian virtue has strayed away from adopting the names of biblical women and has extended towards adorning a baby daughter with the name of a much-coveted feminine virtue: hence *Temperance, Prudence, Faith, Grace,* and even, in one case we have been alerted to, *Silence.* To saddle a girl with a name that is wont to single her out, or even to place her in some degree of local renown, is to make her journey into demure feminine obscurity all the harder.

Beware too the titillations of literature: *Roxanne* may sound alluring, for example, but that is precisely why Mr Defoe selected it as an appropriate name for one of loose morals, such as the heroine of his novel, *Roxana.* Let this serve as an illustration of the menace that so often loiters in the pages of too much imaginative literature. If you insist on reading fiction, at least have the discipline to abstain from allowing its subject matter to spill over into your everyday life.

Finally, a warning against the overuse of the diminutive form of many female names. Many Elizabeths have passed their childhood accustomed to being addressed by their immediate kin as *Betsy.* This is a tolerable term of endearment, as long as it is confined to the privacy of the family home. But no family of respectable society should ever contemplate *christening* their daughter with such a girlish diminutive! Though so many innocent qualities are admirable when carried into womanhood, a childhood name is not one of them. Christen your daughters with a complete and correct name, though by all means you may choose to indulge them in private with your 'Pollys' and your 'Bettys', whilst still in infancy. But when girl becomes woman, she must leave these girlish whimsies in the nursery, along with her dolls and jump ropes.

INSPIRED BY NINETEENTH-CENTURY BABY-NAMING TRENDS

How to Use a Milk Catcher

'THE PROTECTORS ARE DESIGNED TO SURROUND AND HOLD
FIRM THE ENTIRE BREAST, LENDING A MOST GRATIFYING
SILHOUETTE, AND THE SUPPLENESS OF THE RUBBER WILL
NOT BRUISE YOUR MATERNAL BLESSINGS.'

As every mother has learned to her great cost, the handling and nursing of a newborn is an exhausting and onerous task. One may venture to state that it is indeed most *unnatural* to be so closely confined to a child as to have to exclude oneself from the pleasures and comforts of society. Surely a lady is entitled to go abroad on occasion? Surely it is her *duty* to bestow the pleasure of her company upon all who deserve to receive it? To nurse a newborn oneself is an inconvenience beyond all consideration and as such can prevent a lady of high standing from enjoying her happiest and most influential years.

Is it not as well for a child to become accustomed early on to nourishment other than that provided by its *mother's* founts? Are new mothers not already weighed down by fatigue and womanly complaints which nursing a newborn would surely increase? The agreeable practice of employing a wet nurse to deal with such trifles has, of late, worked most admirably. The milk of a judiciously chosen wet nurse provides an adequate degree of sustenance, and giving a child over to be nursed benefits the mother greatly, as it prevents her from becoming unduly weakened by the demands of a ravenous infant.

Alas! How fickle is fashion that it now dictates it is the mother *herself* who must bear the burden of feeding her own child. Indeed, the requirement is such that for a mother to be truly admired she must nurse the child at her *own bosom*. It seems that all eminent physicians are now in agreement that the mother's milk is the most appropriate food for an infant during the first months of its life. That by feeding one's own child, a bond can be built that will prove most advantageous to the little suckler's health!

It is of course your *duty* to submit to the commands of fashion – no lady would wish to bring disgrace upon herself by adhering to outmoded ideas.

Do not despair, however, for we have heard of a cunning device that will enable you to indulge in the current practice of breastfeeding without sacrificing your social ambitions or your toilet.

A woman inventor of outstanding intelligence, most sensitive to the concerns of a nursing mother, has developed a most ingenious and useful milk catcher. Indeed, it has been designed *solely* to avert an abundance of milk from wetting the silk of your dresses, and to improve the form and pert appearance of your globes in a most captivating manner.

The device consists of two breast protectors fashioned

from gutta-percha, that most flexible of natural rubbers harvested from the Gutta trees of Malaya. Indeed, it is the very same material as is used to fashion the nipples of nursing-bottles and the bulbs of breast-pumps.

The protectors are designed to surround and hold firm the entire breast, lending a most gratifying silhouette, and the suppleness of the rubber will not bruise your maternal blessings (such are its sympathetic qualities).

The protective rubber cups are held in place by a clever system of elastic straps which are passed over the shoulders, and from which the cups are suspended by means of flat buttons and buttonholes, and which are in turn held in place by an elastic band around the waist.

It is a most comfortable device which, when fitted in the correct manner, will allow you to go forth into society freed from the anxiety that unwanted leakages may spoil the serenity of your demeanour.

You may wonder that it is a waste for your milky secretions to spill uselessly into a rubber cup, but the resourceful creator has in her wisdom placed a small orifice within each catcher to collect the milk and to allow for subsequent emptying (straight into the mouth of your famished infant, no doubt!).

BASED ON THE 'MILK CATCHER FOR NURSING WOMEN', PATENTED BY LYDIA EMELINE PATTEE, 1884

How to Find Solace in Liquor and Laudanum

'IF A LADY SHOULD SUFFER DAILY WITH NEURALGIA, AS A CONSEQUENCE OF HER DELICATE CONSTITUTION, IRKSOME SERVANTS OR TROUBLESOME OFFSPRING, WHO CAN BLAME HER SHOULD SHE SEE FIT TO RESORT TO OPIUM-EATING ON A DAILY BASIS, SO THAT HER AFFLICTION NOT BE PERMITTED TO INTERFERE WITH HER RESPONSIBILITIES?'

The trials of a mother are myriad. None who are not mothers themselves can guess the torment of keeping house, managing the servants and maintaining all necessary social decorum, whilst seeing to it that one adheres unwearyingly to the hour spent daily with one's offspring. Nonetheless, it can be widely observed that in the normal course of events, a mother will carry out all that is asked of her with apparent ease.

However, a mother is first a woman and will, in addition to her duties, have to withstand the many afflictions common to that title, with all the poise she can manage. The cyclical spasms of the gut, the headaches, neuralgias and distempers of the spirit are all the curse of the fair sex.

How to Find Solace in Liquor and Laudanum

How is it that a lady of refinement can keep all her appointments, be seen abroad in carriage or on foot, keep up with her parlour arts, manage a household, and be a mother to her children, if she is afflicted by ailment at every turn?

There is available an *antidote* to a woman's labours. A heaven-sent, medicinal rescue, that will not only ease physical pain, but will also bring about restorative sleep. The opium pill, known in tincture form as laudanum, is the medicine of choice for ladies of character. It is a wonder-cure for ladies' troubles of all varieties. See that you purchase it from reputable chemists and physicians, as these will supply responsible instructions in its proper consumption.

It is perhaps worthy of note that a lady should not concern herself with talk of the *habit-forming* nature of opium-eating

or laudanum-drinking. It is a *cure*, a *cordial*, intended for the purposes of the *relief of pain* or other medical discomforts. *No cure can be considered habit-forming!* If a lady should suffer *daily* with neuralgia, as a consequence of her delicate constitution, irksome servants or troublesome offspring, who can blame her, should she see fit to resort to opium-eating on a *daily basis,* so that her affliction not be permitted to interfere with her responsibilities?

A mother of delicate sensibility may be troubled with such a severe case of nerves prior to a social engagement, that a drop of laudanum (a most palatable tincture when consumed with quinine and brandy) may be considered *curative* before she leaves her bedchamber. Indeed, a dainty bottle carried about her person *discreetly* may be in order, lest the evening prove vexing. (It may be considered *advantageous* to be troubled with nerves upon the occasion of a visit to the opera, or an orchestral concert: opium can have a most agreeable effect when listening to music.)

The calmative effects of both liquor and laudanum have not been lost upon those we employ to nurse our infants. A diluted dram of gin or brandy will most effectively soothe a newborn if administered promptly after delivery, and assist greatly in the expulsion of the meconium, where the same has not been naturally excreted during labour.

The first sight of your newborn can be arresting: its feeble appearance prompts most mothers and nurses to feel moved to administer a cordial. In such cases, wine mixed with milk or diluted pap can be most restorative.

In 'Godfrey's Cordial', laudanum is combined with

caraway seeds, brandy and treacle, and is a medicine most vital in the treatment of infantile colic. It acts as a carminative, purging the gut of wind and obstructions (and proves equally efficacious in fluxes and intestinal complaints in older children and adults). Moreover, if you resist the temptation to have a nurse suckle your infant, opting instead to offer it your own breast, Godfrey's Cordial can bring about a dampening of its appetite, sufficient to enable you to enjoy a healthful night's sleep without fear of disturbance.

This brand is most easily come by. Its distinctive glass bottle, corked in a thin neck, is filled upon the counter by the pharmacist, from a jug which he mixes himself. Be sure to instruct your woman assiduously in the purchasing of it: the mixture that is decanted from the very dregs of the jug is most likely to have been sitting there a while. The opiate will be greatly increased in strength in these portions and means that a small drop will have as powerful an effect upon your infant as a larger dose.

Caution is in order, should your woman send a child to run your errand to the chemist. The urchins of the deserving poor have been sedated from birth by Godfrey's Cordial and cannot resist its pull. We have heard from many a household where the chemist's bill has been doubled by the imps who drain the bottle dry even before they reach the scullery door, whereupon someone has to be sent out a second time for more.

All those who harbour a suspicion that the nurse in their employ is indolent and idle would be wise to ascertain from their local druggist the quantities of syrup of poppy purchased on her account. Many a healthful babe has perished from such a heinous over-reliance on 'The Quietness'.

INSPIRED BY AN ANONYMOUS ARTICLE IN *THE CATHOLIC WORLD*, SEPTEMBER 1881, BEMOANING THE EVILS OF ENGLISH AND AMERICAN OPIUM ABUSE

How to Hire a Nursemaid

'YOU MUST SEEK OUT A YOUNG WOMAN OF IMPECCABLE CHARACTER WHO IS BLESSED WITH A FOND DISPOSITION TOWARDS ALL STICKY NURSLINGS.'

Every mother of distinction must take great pains when procuring for herself a nursemaid. Such a creature is an indispensable necessity for every good lady encumbered with offspring. A responsible nursemaid will undertake all duties pertaining to the young, from weaning onwards, leaving you free from burdens and able to pursue all your vital social engagements. A nursemaid will have charge of the *whole nursery*, to which you will be required to make only one daily visit, should you be not otherwise occupied.

To this end, you must seek out a young woman of impeccable character who is blessed with a fond disposition towards all sticky nurslings. Look for a young girl of no more than twenty years, possessed of a fair degree of cleverness and with a face unlikely to cause panic. She must be brimful of patience and most agreeable of temper. Her manners must be pure and her cleanliness precise. She ought to be full of truthfulness, obedient of nature and be somewhat acquainted with the skills of ironing and of the needle. A good nursemaid will be practised in the art of holding an infant in the correct manner, that is to say, she will not always hold it upright pressed close to her chest so that the child's stomach becomes uncomfortably compressed. She will refrain at most times from pulling the infant up by its arms and should take care that any of the little accidents that must inevitably occur are not the result of neglect.

We have heard at times of such nursemaids as would conceal certain accidents, for fear of incurring the displeasure and indignation of the parents. Indeed, one little unfortunate received a dislocation of the thigh bone which her nursemaid, by clever pretence, concealed from the parents for such a length of time that the poor child was never able to recover. For this reason, never be churlish to your nursemaid, but be at all times pleasant, that she may have no reason to leave you unacquainted with your child's progress.

It is desirable that you choose a nursemaid of great observation and one that has some degree of acquaintance with the diseases of childhood that she may be familiar with the symptoms of measles, whooping cough, worms and dentition. Better still, that she be versed in the simple remedies useful in the aforementioned ailments. A nursemaid should be of such robust constitution that she is able to rise from her bed at all hours of the night to attend to her charges and still be of a sunny disposition the following day. She must be content to reside in the nursery, taking her every meal with the children and sleeping close by them.

How to Hire a Nursemaid

A nursemaid's general duties will include the washing and dressing of all infants, the seeing to their every meal, and the overseeing of the daily constitutional (weather permitting). She will teach children of the correct age how to walk, taking care to guide by hand, but never favouring one hand above the other to avoid pulling a little shoulder out of place. She should take it upon herself to break any infant of its bad habits, that they may not display such evils when visiting upon their parents. Finger sucking and nose picking are two such habits that may be broken by the patience and perseverance of a good nursemaid. She must never inflict a punishment on these occasions, unless you are of a mind to allow her such privileges, in which case you may provide her with a good leather nursery strap or spanking paddle. A good and faithful nursemaid will repeat to you all the defects she observes in your children that they may be properly checked and eradicated at once. In this way may a nursemaid earn the respect of her charges.

When you find yourself in need of such a wench, simply place a short advertisement in a respected newspaper:

Wanted, a steady nursemaid. Apply at . . .

Or

Wanted, young girl to take care of child two years old.
Apply at . . .

You will find that you receive a glut of young girls at your door from which to make your choice. Ensure that you choose one of good country stock, who is sober, trustworthy and imbued with that rare talent of amusing children without succumbing to the most frightful of boredoms.

INSPIRED BY CHAPTERS IN *THE BOOK OF HOUSEHOLD MANAGEMENT* BY MRS ISABELLA BEETON, 1861

How to Save Your Infant's Soul by Controlling Its Motions

'FROM BIRTH A MOTHER SHOULD INSTRUCT HER NURSE
TO EXAMINE THE PATTERN BY WHICH THE INFANTILE
EVACUATIONS OCCUR THAT SHE MAY BECOME A FAMILIAR
EXPERT IN THE MOTIONS OF THE TENDER INFANT
IN HER CHARGE.'

Cleanliness and a suppression of all base human elements are essential to good motherhood, as they set apart the great and the genteel from the common and the polluted. A child cannot be left to struggle alone against its animalisms: without a mother's guidance, it will surely fall victim to all those urges that so debauch the offspring of the ruffian.

A fine mother has a duty to embark upon a campaign to control her infant's movements and ablutions from the very earliest days. For it is in the base gratification an infant experiences at these times, that a fledgling connection is set up in that delicate mind between things foul and debauched and all personal satisfactions. Conquer and control these movements early on and you will set free his mind and soul to become filled with a spotless purity of

spirit that will stand him in good stead for the entire duration of his life.

This process cannot be begun too early. From birth a
mother should instruct her nurse to examine the pattern
by which the infantile evacuations occur, noting the interval
after feeding and the frequency through the day and night.
In this way may she become a familiar expert in the motions
of the tender infant in her charge, so that she may rapidly
come to anticipate them at every turn.

The infant must be cleansed thoroughly in warm water,
which is turned steadily colder by degrees as the days pass
and the infant's strength and constitution grow. Careful
attention must be paid to the thorough drying of the skin,
in particular, in the cases of fat infants, to those folds of skin
which are wont to be secreted away, and which will rapidly
fall victim to troublesome excoriations and sores. A fine
dusting of starch or of wig-powder may be of great assistance here. We would urge all mothers of refinement to be
wary of the pins by which their nurses secure the infant's
napkin. These pins, in the hands of careless nurses, are oft
the cause of injurious impact upon the bellies and groins of
our precious offspring.

Assuage any fears you have that your nurse may indulge in
that abhorrent practice, so favoured by the squalid masses,
of leaving soiled napkins by the fireplace to dry, to be then
reused without ever having been washed out thoroughly. By
such rank neglect will your infant be persuaded to revel in
a fetidness of body and mind. It will risk his moral undoing!
See that you are certain she exercises a stringent hygiene
at all times and in all things. She must change his napkin at

every emptying of bladder and bowel. The shirt, petticoat, dress and stockings must be changed and laundered daily. There can be no permitted exceptions.

A holed chair will now become your most essential item of nursery furniture. See that all efforts are made to ensure the infant's comfort. A hot brick, replaced whenever the heat drops off, should be housed in a place beneath the seat. This will maintain the bodily warmth of the infant for the (long) duration of his time on the chair. The hole will enable all matter and liquids to fall into a chamber pot below. He should be fixed into a seated position on the chair, by way of specially designed straps that will keep him from slumping or falling. As he grows more mobile, the straps will also prevent him from vacating the chair until you are satisfied he is done.

How to Save Your Infant's Soul By Controlling Its Motions

By this method you will teach him to notify you intelligently, in advance of his bodily needs, thereby reducing the duration of the day he spends strapped into the chair. By the age of three months or so, you may be assured that you will have no further need of napkins at all. Above all, you will have instructed your infant in the very earliest lesson by which it will come to see that it is *its mother's will and not its own* that must govern its every bodily action and mental thought. For only then can you be assured of his respectability in this life, and his salvation in the next.

INSPIRED BY THE LATE-NINETEENTH-CENTURY TENDENCY
TOWARDS VERY EARLY TOILET TRAINING

How to Look to the Fateful Consequences of Bad Wet Nursing

'ALTHOUGH MANY HAVE BEEN RAISED TO GOOD HEALTH
UPON THE SUCKLING OF A GOAT, THERE ARE NONE THAT WE
KNOW OF WHO HAVE ACHIEVED A GREATER STATUS IN LIFE
THAN THAT OF A FOOTMAN.'

A lady of high breeding knows that the distasteful practice of suckling one's own child is to be avoided at all costs. It is ruinous to the figure, noisome to one's dress and interferes most unreasonably with a necessary quantity of gadding about. Furthermore, you will find that many husbands (of virile stock and anxious for many heirs) will not be content to suffer it: the practice renders one infertile and of little use in the marital bed for as long as one continues to indulge. No, it is better by far that you seek out a willing young wench of favourable background who would be most glad to offer the services of her brimming globes in exchange for board and lodgings.

See to it that you engage only the most suitable of wenches – one whose character is unblemished by immoral acts and whose temperament is as gentle and good as if she were your child's very mother. Avoid those disreputable souls that would abandon or suffocate their own infant to gain a position in your household; only consider those who have lost a child by *natural* means. The best of wet nurses will be pleasant of face with neither spots nor scars to render her alarming to a babe. She should be robust of body and have suffered from no syphilitic or injurious illness. See that she does not own tresses of a reddish hue that hide an untrustworthy and fiery character and that she does not harbour any hint of deformity. A limp or a squint or a troublesome way with words tells only of a weakness you would not wish to be passed through to your own child.

Assure yourself that the milk on offer is of the most respectable quality. It should be of creamy thickness and whitish hue, not thin and blue or yellow and sluggish. It should taste sweet and palatable with no hint of sourness: you may bid a prospective wet nurse to release a quantity of her supply upon a plate, that you may sample the quality and judge for yourself. Once satisfied with your choice, you may install her in the nursery along with your child and seek out the comforts of society for yourself once more. You must forbid her to lay with your child at night, for too much beer at supper has sent many a child to the grave suffocated by an intoxicated nurse!

You may find it at times troublesome to house a wet nurse at such close quarters. The cries of your child at night may still be heard echoing along the corridors and may disturb your sleep in a most vexing manner. If this be the case, you may prefer to have your child sent out to be suckled at a nurse's own lodgings until at least he is weaned.

You must be vigilant in your searches, however, for many an infant has come to a sticky end as a consequence of bad and neglectful wet nursing. Be sure to inspect the lodgings, that they are clean and not overrun with an army of snotty children. Be sure, too, that there are no goats on the premises, as many *country* wet nurses are wont to call upon the assistance of these creatures when their own milk is too much in demand. Although many have been raised to good health upon the suckling of a goat, there are none that we know of who have achieved a greater status in life than that of a footman.

Beware too of engaging a wet nurse through the enticing words of advertisements. There are many such notices in our newspapers which upon first reading appear most faultless.

NURSE CHILD WANTED: the Advertiser, a young, respectable, married woman with a little family of her own, nice country home, would be glad to accept the charge of an infant. If sickly would receive a parent's care. Terms, Fifteen shillings a month; or would adopt entirely for the small sum of Twelve pounds.

These innocently worded lies are the sticky traps of Baby Farmers. Luring you in, with their honeyed words and promises, to care for a child as if it were their own, they are moved by the devil himself to leave a babe to slowly starve to death before wrapping its body in newspaper and throwing it into the river. These 'Angel Makers' are rife, condemning a child to death for mere profit, and fit only to be hunted down and executed. Be sure you do not fall for their practised deceit.

INSPIRED BY THE CASE OF THE READING BABY FARMER, AMELIA DYER, EXECUTED IN 1896 FOR THE MURDER OF A BABY GIRL AND SUSPECTED OF KILLING AND DISPOSING OF AT LEAST 50 OTHER BABIES

How to Use the Anodyne Necklace

'THE OFFSPRING OF MANY AN EARL AND BARON HAVE
BEEN SAVED FROM THE BRINK OF THE GRAVE, THEIR
CONVULSIONS, FEVERS, GRIPES AND LOOSE BOWELS MET
WITH AN ABRUPT END AFTER THE SIMPLE DONNING OF THIS
MIRACULOUS NECKLACE.'

The peril of an infant's first dentition cannot be emphasised enough. Of all the hazards which may endanger an infant's life, teething is the most commonly feared. Some great medical authorities have placed the mortality rate of teething infants as high as *one sixth* of all those who suffer it. It is with this in mind that we herein offer some few hints and clues on how best to diminish the associated risks.

Firstly, see to it that you are familiar with your child's gums. Look for swellings therein, along with a reddening of the cheeks (caused by an increase in blood to the head) and a raging thirst. Loose bowels and skin rashes often accompany the process but should not be checked: they are a *necessary* means by which nature avoids yet greater horrors.

These symptoms are consistent with the state of Natural

Teething, which can be most easily managed. Offer the infant the breast in short but frequent intervals. Apply gentle pressure or friction to the area of swelling. Liquorice or orris-root that have been well stripped, or else coral or ivory rings, are useful in applying a little pressure to the gums when chewed upon, and thereby offer some comfort to the distressed infant.

An intensely red and furious swelling of the gum, along with copious slavering, irritable eyes, burning cheeks, a high fever and an unquenchable thirst are cause for far greater alarm. These are the chief symptoms of *Difficult Dentition,* and should strike terror into the hearts of every mother and nurse who has the misfortune to be witness to them. Call immediately for a physician, for the swollen gum must be lanced cleanly through, with the lancet being plunged into the very heart of the swelling. See that the infant's head is bathed morning and night in cold water and that its diet is restricted.

Some nurses may advise the use of peony root or, worse still, the dried root of henbane. This last carries the foul stench of witchery and such a nurse as would recommend it should be driven from the nursery and from your home. The power of this plant is great indeed: even the leaves have cast a spell over the pure of heart so that they cannot stand erect for the giddy fits that overcome them. Whatever may be the good effects of this upon cutting a tooth must be outweighed by the risk of the infant sucking upon the root. So great is its poison, it would surely result in death.

With this fate never far from a mother's mind, one may

find genteel assurance from the satisfied clientele of Dr Paul Chamberlen, who has devised and investigated the beaded Anodyne Necklace. Never before has there been made available to a respectable mother a necklace that offers such *complete protection* and peace of mind. The offspring of many an Earl and Baron have been saved from the brink of the grave, their convulsions, fevers, gripes and loose bowels coming to an abrupt end after the simple donning of this miraculous necklace.

For such a miracle a mother of means would surely pay handsomely. The Anodyne Necklace is priced fairly at the cost of 5 shillings, merely the weekly wages of the average man. See that you make your purchase only from a reputable outlet. The authors have found great satisfaction from the gentlewoman up one pair of stairs at the sign of the sugar loaf (a confectioner's worthy of mention), alongside Old Round Court, near the New Exchange in the Strand, London.

A word of caution: for those among you who take *The Weekly Journal*, we would urge you to desist! Therein was to be discovered a most scandalous misrepresentation of the respectable Anodyne Necklace in March 1717. Dr Chamberlen was much wronged by accusations of having made false claims and of constructing his necklaces from the *beaded skulls of indifferent persons!* This heinous editorial urged its readers to respond to the necklace with *vehement curse and reproach*. We too feel most insistent upon this matter: we urge you, our most respected readers, to pay no heed to this falsehood. Take comfort from the knowledge that, in providing your infant with this beaded wonder, you are in the honoured company of some of the greatest aristocratic families in our land!

INSPIRED BY THE ADVERTISING WARS IN QUACK MEDICINE IN THE EARLY DECADES OF THE EIGHTEENTH CENTURY, AND ADAPTED IN PART FROM ORIGINAL DENTAL ADVICE IN *THE MATERNAL MANAGEMENT OF CHILDREN IN HEALTH AND DISEASE* BY THOMAS BULL, MD, 1840

How to Use a Bubby Pot

'A CHILD FED ON MORE STIMULATING NOURISHMENT THAN A MOTHER'S OWN MILK WILL SURELY THRIVE AND MAY EVEN SURVIVE 'TIL ADULTHOOD.'

It is most advantageous for a mother to accustom her child early on to the benefits of *artificial feeding*. Not only will the demands upon the mother be less relentless and gruelling, but her child will sleep for longer if fed on substances slow to digest. This in turn leads to quieter nights and releases the mother from her shackles to take her pleasure in society in the knowledge that means other than maternal milk are ready at hand to sustain her child. It is also true that a child nourished in such a manner will acquire a stronger constitution, enabling it to resist, *to a greater degree*, the diseases and sicknesses so prevalent in infancy. A mother's milk, although at times convenient, is often affected by the fatigue and anxiety of the mother, thereby losing much of its beneficial qualities.

We wish to impress upon the minds of all inexpert mothers that there are many cases of infantile rickets or fatal diseases which could be *entirely* avoided by rearing a child by hand. That is to say that a child fed on more stimulating nourishment than a mother's own milk will surely thrive and may even survive 'til adulthood.

One may presume that the rearing of a child by hand would be fraught with difficulties and anxieties. We would beg to differ. The extra work required is only in the preparation of the food, and a reliable nursemaid will find it of very little inconvenience. The few articles required for the correct feeding of an infant are a lamp with which to keep the food warm at night, a bubby pot or a pap boat and a small pap saucepan for use during the day. It is to the talents of a certain Dr Hugh Smith that we must owe our unerring gratitude, for it is his invention of the humble bubby pot which has served to release innumerable women from the tyrannies of the breast and the wet-nurse. This most simple of devices resembles a teapot made of pewter, but mothers of good taste may obtain it in silver or porcelain tastefully decorated in the most fetching of manners. Its perforated spout need only be covered with cloth (to serve as a nipple) and through it your infant may obtain its nourishment. The good doctor states most knowledgably that, 'The infant is obliged to labour for every drop he receives.'

Although we would recommend the bubby pot over the more commonly used pap boat, we would not insist *you* prefer one to the other. The pap boat, which resembles most closely a gravy boat, is more easily obtained and can be found in the cleverest of designs, most often in the shape of a duck, which will afford delighted amusement to your infant. That they both achieve the same purpose, of delivering sustenance to your child, is our only true concern.

The nourishing mixture known as pap is the food we highly recommend you raise your infant upon. What could be easier to prepare than bread and flour made liquid in a quantity of water? Moreover, what child could want for better nourishment from the moment of its birth? If your child seems not satisfied on such a mixture, you may increase its nourishment by adding a little butter and milk, or indeed by substituting the milk for broth. We recommend that you always add some loaf sugar to render the gruel most palatable and strengthening. Many have found that varying the ingredients to include raw meat juices, wine, beer, arrowroot, semolina or Castille soap has proved most successful.

The pap should be cooked in such quantity as to last a day and night and once cooled should be the consistency of a custard. One or two spoonfuls should be placed in the pap saucepan as needed, with enough cow's milk or water added to render the mixture as cream. It should be heated gently (upon the lamp during the night) then poured into the bubby pot, then the spout may be placed in the infant's mouth for him to draw the liquid out. Half a pot at a time will be quite sufficient for the first two months of an infant's life, thereafter you may wish to add an egg to the preparation for extra thickness.

In this manner may your infant be most healthfully raised and you may be sure to keep him well beyond his third year.

How to Use a Bubby Pot

BASED ON THE HISTORY OF INFANT FEEDING AND THE
INVENTION OF THE BUBBY POT IN 1770 BY DR HUGH SMITH

74

How to Produce a Son and Heir

'A WOMAN IS COMMONLY UNDER GREAT PRESSURE TO SEE THAT SHE CONTINUE RISKING HER HEALTH AND SANITY BY ALLOWING HER REPEATED IMPREGNATION, IN ORDER THAT A BOY, THAT MOST INFERIOR SEX, MAY BE BEGOTTEN.'

There can be little doubt of the pre-eminence of the female sex above the male. As odd as this may sound, it being so contrary to all established wisdom, it is but a trifle to demonstrate this to be fact. One need only look on that angelic countenance that is peculiar to Woman, and oh so infrequently evident in the look of men. Man, after all, was created out of the Earth itself, as are all common creatures. Woman was created out of a Radiant Beam of Light and, for her miraculous creation, was Man maimed, for ever after missing a rib. Moreover, Man will remain ever incomplete, unless he is granted the grace of a *permanent union with Woman*, in which his loss would be retrieved and he would be made whole once more.

It is from a woman that we are most likely to perceive that dazzling splendour of Paradise – in the perfect arch of her eyebrow, her tender flesh, her soft and glittering locks with which Cupid threads his bow, her sparkling eyes and snow-white neck. In the rosy portals of her captivating smile, parted softly to reveal rows of pearl-white teeth (fewer in number than in a man for they are called upon more to nibble delicately than to chomp and grind like an animal), in the swell of her breasts, two snow-covered mountains of delight, and the whole grace and symmetry of her person, in all these things are we presented with a radiant miracle, far greater than any other in God's Creation.

Moreover, should you ever have the misfortune to witness the drowning in the open waters of the sea of both a man and a woman, you will see that the water itself pays homage to this truth. For the man will at once be swallowed and engulfed, like all other gross bodies, plunged forever to the very bottom of the ocean, for it is there that he most belongs. The woman, in contrast, is supported on the surface, held aloft by Nature itself even in her watery grave, as that compassionate element displays its reluctance to bring about the destruction of so much excellence.

No, of woman's pre-eminence over man, there can be no debate.

And yet, as men have come to assert themselves, with much blunder and clatter, over women in society, they endeavour to *counteract and overlook* this natural pre-eminence. Men labour to assert themselves by raising the importance of those base spheres in which they most excel: politics, finance and property. In all these things men attempt to inflate their place on this earth. A consequence of this, that often causes much discomfort for women, is the necessity placed by men upon their wives to produce a *male* infant, who will, under *man's* own law, stand ever after as Son and Heir to his father's estate. A woman is commonly under great pressure to continue risking her health and sanity by allowing her repeated impregnation, in order that a boy, that most *inferior* sex, may be begotten.

Many advocate a programme of rigid diet and exercise prior to breeding, swearing that the husband should indulge himself in nothing but substantial and wholesome food, exercise long and hard in the open, all the while abstaining (and this last, crucially, for some lengthy while) from that peculiar indulgence, until the time is most certain to be conducive to procreating. Such arguments insist that the wife, meanwhile, must eat only foods of a farinaceous nature and exercise daily to the point of fatigue, taking pains to keep the exclusive company of those women older

than herself. There is undeniably much of influence in this regime and it has enjoyed success in as many as half of those couples who have adhered to its precepts. But there are inevitably those few men for whom such a recommendation is not adequate, and for whom more certain guarantees are sought.

To this end, may we recommend the adoption of a method much tried and tested by the French aristocracy – that of removing the left testicle? The ancients knew well that it is the right testicle that will create a boy and the left that produces a girl. They would oft tie off the left bag, so as to restrict the flow of female seed from therein. However, the French have determined that by its *complete removal*, the left testicle would be forever prohibited from the planting of a female. If you equip your husband with this information, it will either grant him the means with which to satisfy any *earnest* desires he harbours for that highly prized son or else hush him into a quiet satisfaction that he has hitherto been blessed with precious daughters.

ADAPTED, IN PART, FROM *FEMALE PRE-EMINENCE, OR THE DIGNITY AND EXCELLENCE OF THAT SEX ABOVE THE MALE* BY HENRY CORNELIUS AGRIPPA, 1670

How to Keep Healthful
with Hydropathy

'THE AFFLICTION OF A FALLEN WOMB CAN BE CURED MOST
EFFICACIOUSLY BY THE TREATMENT OF INVIGORATION TO
THE WHOLE OF THE AFFECTED REGION.'

Such are the demands made upon a new mother that it is of vital importance she keep a robust health and an unfailing constitution. Once married and embarked on the process of breeding, a woman is unlikely to go one season without bearing yet another reminder of her husband's needs. The fortitude required for such a wearisome task is so great as to need all available assistance.

But the modern mother has grown tired of the physician's cures: the relentless bleedings, scarifications, cauterising and purging, and the paroxysms of almost intolerable torment brought on by the insertion of leeches into the womb, which relieve neither the suffering of childbirth, the distress of conjugal excess, nor the pain of pelvic diseases!

It is with pleasure and relief, then, that all mothers welcome the discovery made by Vincent Priessnitz, a humble peasant from the mountain village of Grefenberg, who cured himself of broken ribs by wrapping bandages doused in cold mountain water around his afflicted part. He saw fit to develop his method and now a number of enlightened physicians have brought the wondrously curative system of hydropathy to our shores. This treatment of chronic maladies by the exclusive use of cold water has proved to be of great value to the most despairing of mothers.

'Tis in the peaceful and romantic town of Malvern that one may find the very best of hydropathic institutions, much frequented by the wealthiest intelligentsia of society. It is here that many a mother, turned invalid through exhaustion and other complaints peculiar to women, may find a miraculous cure. A husband of good character, and mindful of his reputation, would grant at once his wife's request to travel to such a retreat to partake in such treatments as would restore her to good health. (As such places do not allow the intrusion of children, may we suggest you resign yourself to a most pleasant interlude of childlessness? Indeed, you may wish to prolong your stay, should your malady prove tenacious.)

The benefits of the water-cure are numerous and astounding. Many an emaciated and helpless woman has been brought back to vigorous well-being by the treatments at their disposal. A successful restoration will require that you are immersed frequently in baths of almost intolerably low temperatures, spend much time wrapped in cold damp sheets and consume innumerable glasses of icy water (drunk freely as a common beverage throughout the day). You need not fear catching cold from plunging into the freezing baths immediately upon leaving the warmth of your bed, indeed the brusque transition of temperature soothes the nerves and revives the beauty of feminine skin.

The affliction of a fallen womb can be cured most efficaciously by the treatment of *invigoration* to the whole of the affected region. A quantity of wet bandages, most carefully and tightly applied, along with frequent injections of cold water into the feminine canal and douching of the pelvic area until the patient experiences a *release* of tension, has brought relief to many of those suffering from this most common of childbirth disabilities.

But it is to the process of childbirth itself that hydropathy lends itself most effectively. You should immerse yourself in a tub of cold water, commonly known as a *sitz* bath, when the pains of labour are at their most intense and you will find the water has an invigorating, yet calming effect, reducing your pains to the merest feelings of pressure. An enema of cold water, given at this point, will soothe you into a quiet sleep in preparation for the trials ahead. You should return to the water an hour after the child is born and allow your abdomen to be wrapped in a quantity of cold, wet towels. You will find this treatment enables you to rise from your bed as early as the third day after delivery and strengthens you to walk abroad in the fresh air! You must cover your face, however, so as not to alarm any acquaintances who might see you about so soon.

Even the most delicate of women have become so passionately attached to the cures of hydropathy as to have installed all necessary equipment in their own homes! The most popular apparatus is the ascending douche, the head of which should be placed at a height appropriate to your requirements, the pipe being of good size to allow the gushing column of water to be both strong and voluminous.

BASED ON THE HISTORY OF HYDROPATHY, ONE OF A NUMBER OF ALTERNATIVE CURATIVE SYSTEMS POPULARISED IN THE EARLY NINETEENTH CENTURY

How to Use Fruit Judiciously

'ALL FRUIT, EVEN IN THE MOST FRESH AND PERFECT OF
STATES, IS OF DOUBTFUL BENEFIT AND INDEED, MANY
FRUITS CAN PROVE MOST INJURIOUS TO THE HEALTH OF A
CHILD.'

The correct nourishment of a child is an onerous task for all keen mothers, and it is a wise mother indeed who takes note of the advice given by the knowledgeable scientists of the day. These learned physicians, who have studied closely the immature digestive system of the infant, have been drawn to the most valuable of conclusions: all fruit, even in the most fresh and perfect of states, is of doubtful benefit and, indeed, many fruits can prove entirely injurious to the health of a child.

A large proportion of physicians have noted that the deadly cholera seems to make its attack immediately after the consumption of fruit and, although other physicians argue that this is purely accidental and that only an *excess* of these delights could prove so hurtful, you are well advised to practise caution when allowing such indulgences to be included in the diet of your infant.

How to Use Fruit Judiciously

Many would believe that summer fruits are the cause of childhood diseases, since the most fateful illnesses prevail at the time of year when these fruits are at their most abundant. We would therefore urge you to take proper care when making your selection.

There are certain fruits that should never be given to children: melons, peaches, plums and grapes all have the most tempting of flavours but the most unwholesome of juices. An enlightened mother would see to it that her child be *entirely unaware* of the existence of any of these forbidden enticements.

It may be acceptable, on occasion, to allow a child to consume a small amount of cherries, gooseberries, strawberries and currants. These seasonal fruits must be at their ripest and upon no account must they be served with cream or sugar as this will render the berries exceedingly agreeable and may encourage a child to consume more than is healthful and to continue to seek out that which will disagree with him.

Most fruits can be digested with only the greatest of difficulty; therefore there is sound reason to follow recommended rules should you decide to permit your infant to indulge in the tastes of Paradise.

No child should be given fruit of any kind until he has grown teeth that will allow him to grind the flesh to pulp, and then only fruits from your own country and from their own season should be considered suitable. On no account should unripe fruit be offered, especially if in a raw or uncooked state. Dried fruits are considerably unwholesome and should never be given to a child, lest you create long-lasting mischief.

How to Use Fruit Judiciously

Never allow your child to partake of fruit upon rising in the morning, or immediately before retiring to bed. Any fruit given should form part of a regular meal and should not be given directly after a full meal. The skins of all fruits should be avoided, also the pith, seeds and stones. Only the smallest amount of fruit should be offered at any given time; an excess is to be avoided at all costs.

Of all the fruits of the world, it is the humble apple which can be considered the least harmful. There is no other fruit which keeps longer in perfection or is easier on the digestion. Indeed, a roasted or baked apple served with warm milk is the only fruit to be recommended as being of possible benefit to a child's health.

ADAPTED FROM ORIGINAL ADVICE GIVEN IN *THE YOUNG MOTHER OR MANAGEMENT OF CHILDREN IN REGARD TO HEALTH* BY WILLIAM A. ALCOTT, 1836

How to Cultivate Sound Sleeping Habits

'WOEFUL IS THE HOUSEHOLD IN WHICH THE MOTHER IS
PRONE TO LATE RISING! WE KNOW OF NO KIND OF FAMILY
MORE MISERABLE (SAVE PERHAPS THAT ONE OR TWO WHICH
ARE BLIGHTED BY A DRUNKEN HUSBAND).'

No aspect of motherhood has been as much neglected
in recent times as that of sound sleep. The discipline of
sleep must be rigidly adhered to at night, in order that you
and your children conduct yourselves to your best possible
degree by day.

Nursing mothers must insist upon a newborn infant
being taken away to bed down with a nursemaid and only
brought to its mother in the early hours so that it may
suckle. The alternative to this method is entirely unthink-
able: a gentle lady should never be subjected to that degree
of sleep deprivation as is often the consequence of a
newborn's arrival, which can only lead to her utter mental
degeneration. It cannot be permitted.

During this time it may be of benefit to aid sound sleep
medicinally. Valerian is a herbal means by which a little rest

may be coaxed. We have found that, all too often, a young mother is exhausted by the stresses imposed upon her by the distant sound of her infant being tended by her nurse, so that something *more* is called for. In this case, a little laudanum, in solution with some small quantity of alcohol, is most efficacious. Try, too, either bromide salts or chloral hydrate, as these 'knock-out drops' will induce a restorative sleep in half an hour; less if taken in combination with strong spirits. Fret not that you are resorting to unnatural means in order to gain the rest you deserve: the stresses of early motherhood are in themselves an unnatural state for a lady of refined and delicate persuasion. One must look *beyond nature* in order to redress that natural balance.

Once a child has reached the age of four or five, it is expected to go without its daytime nap, and thereafter sleep soundly for twelve or fourteen hours. Schoolboys will usually require about ten hours' sleep. At this juncture, it is vital that you instil upon your child the importance of early rising. It is true that no mother, nor any other adult, should ever intervene in the natural sleep of a child, adhering strictly to a regular bedtime no matter what evening soirée may be better graced by a capricious exhibition of a young Miss's pianoforte prowess, or a young Sir's poetical recitation. However, by the same token, once a child has come to stir at sunrise, or immediately before, he should be encouraged to rouse himself *instantly*, never opting instead to remain for just a second or two longer. For a second becomes a minute, becomes five, and in the brief close of an eyelid, another hour after sunrise has passed by. He who gives way to the feeling of lying in *just a second longer*, will not thereafter shake off that sluggardly demeanour.

In this, as in all things, a mother must lead by example. Woeful is the household in which the mother is prone to late rising! We know of no kind of family more miserable (save perhaps that one or two which are blighted by a drunken husband). The mother is inevitably deficient in her ability to exercise a strong will, and is plagued with regret throughout the whole day so that her subsequent fretfulness is irksome in the extreme to her husband. Furthermore, her husband is made habitually miserable in consequence of his disturbed (even, in some cases, delayed) breakfast, so that a quarrelsome household is most often the result. The final consequence must surely be upon the children, who are submerged in a perpetual *malcontent*, and are invariably late risers themselves, and are in turn prone to all the ill-temper, ill-discipline and peevishness that is a part of that condition.

In short, sleep must be made the utmost priority in every respectable family, including adhering rigidly to set bedtimes for children, and a prompt and unerring early-rising regime for every member of the household. Nothing must be allowed to interfere with this policy. For the family that fails in it will rapidly fall into ill-health and ill-discipline, with all the consequent ruin to their reputation that must surely ensue.

ADAPTED IN PART FROM ORIGINAL ADVICE FROM WILLIAM A. ALCOTT'S *THE YOUNG WIFE*, 1842, AND HIS LATER TITLE *THE BOY'S GUIDE TO USEFULNESS*, 1844

How to Make a Pudding Cap

'IT IS ESSENTIAL YOU SEE TO IT THAT YOUR CHILD'S SKULL
IS FULLY CUSHIONED THROUGHOUT HIS MOST VULNERABLE
YEARS; A PUDDING CAP IS THE VERY BEST CONTRIVANCE
WITH WHICH TO PRESERVE THE INNOCENT FROM INJURY
WHENEVER IT MAY FALL.'

Every admirable mother is equipped with the desire to protect her offspring from whatever dangers may come its way, and what child can be more in need of protection than the little savage who, in his second year, has found his feet and is practising a newly acquired gait in a manner most comical to behold? He is much like a cock-eyed sot who has drunk his fill of wine and become unsteady on his feet!

As a wise and concerned mother, you will already have sewn a set of leading strings onto the shoulders of your gambolling infant's gown and, as with an over-excited puppy, the strings will enable you to pull your child away from mischief and to lift him clear of the ground whenever he tumbles. As a woman of society, however, you cannot be holding constantly your child's strings, indeed you will have far more important duties with which to fill your day. Your frolicking youngster must be put into the care and trust of its older brothers and sisters and you must see to it that the safety and preservation of its health is always at the forefront of your mind.

A child of such tender years is possessed of the softest of skulls. A knock to the head upon falling can lead to permanent damage, and frequent falls of this nature have been known to scramble the brains to the consistency of pudding, rendering a child forever a dullard or 'pudding head'. It is essential you see to it that your child's skull is fully cushioned throughout his most vulnerable years; a pudding cap is the *very best* contrivance with which to preserve the innocent from injury whenever it may fall.

It is useful to supply your child with an everyday pudding cap, which can be most basic in appearance. It will suffice to line and stuff a band of fabric with horsehair which can be tied around your child's forehead and should be worn over a biggins (a child's close-fitting linen cap that keeps a steady heat round its brain and which prevents other headwear from being dirtied by its mop of sticky hair).

When presenting your child in public, it is fitting for it to be seen wearing a pudding cap of a more luxurious nature. Has it not been told that little Lord Fitzmaurice was spied wearing a pudding cap fashioned from the self-same fabric as his rose-coloured damask coat and trimmed in the most delightful of manners with a display of black and white feathers?

Purchase a length of fabric sufficient for your needs. A glazed cotton or heavy silk would be most desirable. Cut a band of said fabric to measure the full circumference of your child's head. Sew this band into a tube and stuff it with horsehair. The finished roll should resemble a loosely stuffed sausage. Take care not to over-stuff, as the sausage will not sit happily upon the head.

Attach four lightly padded triangular flaps of fabric to the roll so that they may partially cover the top of the head. These flaps may be fastened together by lengths of ribbon and the pudding cap itself may be fastened horizontally around the head and then under the chin. Take care to trim in an eye-catching manner by making much use of velvet, fur, silks and feathers. You may then rest at ease, certain in the knowledge that your little one may stagger to his heart's content, crashing into furniture and hurtling to the floors, without once endangering the family intelligence.

THE PUDDING CAP WAS A FORM OF PROTECTIVE HEADWEAR
WORN BY TODDLERS UP TO THE END OF THE 1700s

How to Select the Correct Companions for Your Child

'SHOULD YOUR CHILD EVER HAPPEN UPON A SNUB NOSE,
SEEN IN CONJUNCTION WITH SMALL, SHELL-LIKE EARS,
A ROSEBUD MOUTH AND NEARSIGHTED EYES, GRAB HER
FIRMLY BY THE WRIST AND FLEE, FOR BOTH YOUR SAKES!'

Mothers, we implore you to take up a close scrutiny of the society your child keeps from the earliest age. In the supervision of this one must proceed with as much urgency as when one oversees the fresh laundering of his bed linen or the delicate management of his diet. It is undeniable that a cheerful disposition is vital to a child's continued good health: what better way can there be of creating and maintaining joviality than to be exposed to generous society from the start? Furthermore, how much more urgent is this in cases where a child exhibits a natural tendency toward diffidence and timidity? A mother who labours to create a sociable child can gain satisfaction from the fact that in doing so she has also safeguarded his manners, mind and morals.

Let us not allow ourselves to be lulled into a false belief that requiring your child to socialise with others will, *of itself*, bring about all desired good effects. The bonds formed in childhood are often carried to the grave: these can be of enormous influence. It is vital that a mother select her child's companions with the utmost care and caution. The right companion can foster habits of cleanliness and neatness better than any other method.

With this aim in mind, we herein seek to enlighten you in the ways of the modern science of physiognomy, which is to say, *how to read the character of the girl by reading her face*. When you have perfected this method, similar techniques may be applied to the assessment of a boy's characteristics.

The Teeth

The girl to seek out as a companion for your child has regular sized, pearl-white teeth which she is not shy to display fully in laughing. This, coupled with features that are at least satisfactorily harmonious, is certain assurance of a remarkable degree of mental balance.

The girl who fixes firm her lips, even when smiling, and thereby reveals very little of her teeth, is certain to have a notable degree of concentration and resolution, and is therefore a wise choice of companion for the mother who seeks to counterbalance a child who flits about.

Those whose teeth display a tendency to lean in towards the mouth from the line of the gum are a good selection to socialise with a child who is reckless and lacking in self-discipline: such girls will surely prove impeccably prudent in money matters.

The Chin

Look out for a round, ample and well-formed chin which denotes a sweet obliging nature. Also promising is the girl with the square, be-dimpled chin: a firm and capable helpmeet. Shun at all costs any with a weak, receding chin: they are base characters and will prove devious, fickle or treacherous.

The Nose

It is our opinion that here, above any other, is the feature with which the character may be accurately assessed. To be most coveted is the Greek nose, whose straight line from base to tip denotes a gentle, peaceable nature, with a love of the arts and of all things beautiful. Such girls are rarely petulant or ill-tempered. When such a nose is coupled with a mouth of generous proportions, you have found a treasure!

The snub-nosed girl will sadly never be a good choice of companion: where the tip is genuinely flattened upon the face she will certainly prove cruel-natured. And should your child ever happen upon a snub-nose, seen in conjunction with small, shell-like ears, a rosebud mouth and nearsighted eyes, grab her firmly by the wrist and flee, for both your sakes! For in such a face is found the very manifestation of callous perfidy.

The Eyes

Large, wide-open eyes, with a clear luminosity, are a sure sign of an affable, tender, constant nature in a young girl. Most mothers would want to avoid striking friendships with a girl with deep-seated eyes, for she is not likely to be fun-loving, nor even tolerant of any joviality. Her leisure hours will most often be spent alone in a darkened room, with only her sombre thoughts for company. Her life is but a serious business!

The long-eyed girl is the corollary of the wide-eyed type. Trust is not within her capabilities: she is forever wary and suspicious. In time, she will grind down your child's good nature with her constant queries and doubts. A friendship not to be indulged.

ADAPTED FROM ORIGINAL ADVICE IN HARRIET HUBBARD AYER'S *A COMPLETE AND AUTHENTIC TREATISE ON THE LAWS OF HEALTH AND BEAUTY*, 1899, AND *THE YOUNG MOTHER, OR MANAGEMENT OF CHILDREN IN REGARD TO HEALTH* BY WILLIAM A. ALCOTT, 1836

How to Minister to the Ailments and Injuries of Childhood

'SUBMERGE THE AFFECTED PART IN ICED WATER AND LEAVE
FOR AS MANY HOURS AS IS PRACTICABLE. IF THE INJURED
JOINT REMAINS WEAK, THEN CONTINUE TO POUR OVER
COLD WATER FROM THE SPOUT OF A TEAKETTLE SEVERAL
TIMES A DAY.'

An infant is a frail and fractious creature, susceptible to all manner of ills and injury. The organisation of its nervous system is most sensitive and leaves a child open to harm from all that surrounds it. The world is full of dangers and no mother, no matter how exemplary, can protect her child from them all. Improper food, cold air, bad air and overheating can all lead to any number of fatal diseases. We propose to lay before you the most common of ailments incidental to childhood, with the proper and most effective cures, that you may endeavour to raise your child to meet its adult years with a robust and healthful constitution.

Inflammation of the Brain

A child who complains of an intense pain in the head and who exhibits a flushed face and a rapid pulse must be suspected of having an inflammation of the brain. It is almost certain to be the case if a child has been exposed too long to the sun, has received a blow to the head or has applied himself too intensely to studying.

Treatment must be rapid, with the patient being bled until he nears fainting. His bowels must be opened with Epsom salts and his head shaved and covered with cloths soaked in iced vinegar. These vigorous measures are required to be repeated as often as is necessary to reduce the inflammation, or death will surely be the consequence.

Bleeding from the Nose

The afflicted infant should be made to sit in an upright position. He should be bled from the arm and iced water should be applied to the back of his neck. If these treatments do not suffice to stem the flow, then a plug of linen moistened with brandy should be fastened to a length of catgut which is to be passed through the nostril, into the throat and drawn out of the mouth, so that the plug blocks the rear nostril.

Sprains

Submerge the affected part in iced water and leave for as many hours as is practicable. If the injured joint remains weak, then continue to pour over cold water from the spout of a teakettle several times a day.

Wounds Poisoned from Bites of Mad Dogs or Rattlesnakes

At the very instant of being bitten, a ligature should be tied most tightly above the wound and the bitten parts of flesh cut directly out. Turpentine should be poured freely into the open wound to excite the inflammation which *must* follow in order to prevent the fatal consequences that would surely ensue if such immediate action were not taken.

Injuries of the Nose and Ear

Clean all the injured parts with clean, fresh water, pull the edges of the wound together as best as you are able and secure them with a few pertinent stitches. If a piece of flesh has become so ripped that it is separated, indeed even if it has been trampled under foot, it may still be placed accurately in its correct position and may yet adhere.

Falling of the Fundament

Many children who cry too frequently or who strain when going to stool, will find themselves afflicted with this uncomfortable ailment. It is correct to treat the gut with warm milk, oak bark and to wash diligently with cold water. The protruding part should be replaced by use of the finger and from then on the child should not be permitted to crouch low when moving his bowels.

Rickets

This disease arises from several causes, the most common being the improper care of infants, by which we mean swaddling them too tightly or loosely and failing to keep them as clean and dry as would be recommended. The disorder becomes apparent around the eighth month and can be recognised by the large floridness of the child's head, its knotty and crooked joints, the swelling of its belly and the waddle of its walk.

An infant so troubled should be fed a light but well-seasoned diet, its limbs arranged to their proper situation by means of tight bandages, and its back rubbed every night with strong rum. Frequent bathing in a cold sea is said to be of immeasurable good use, as is an after-dinner concoction of Peruvian bark and good red wine.

Finally, we would seek to instruct you in the proper application of leeches, most vital in the treatment of many lung diseases, the common childhood croup being but one. Success in the application is rendered more unfailing if the leeches are permitted to first dry out by crawling over clean linen. The body part to be treated should then be made attractive by being moistened with cream, sugar or blood. Once attached, the leeches should be prevented from escape by covering with a wineglass or goblet.

How to Minister to the Ailments and Injuries of Childhood

❦

ADAPTED IN PART FROM *THE HOUSEHOLD CYCLOPEDIA OF GENERAL INFORMATION* BY HENRY HARTSHORNE, MD, 1881

How to Break a Child's Will

'WE HAVE HEARD TELL OF DEVOTED MOTHERS OF
IMAGINATION, MOST WARY OF OVER-INDULGENCE, WHO TIE
THEIR WAYWARD BRATS TO THE LEG OF A KITCHEN TABLE
FOR DAYS ON END.'

Whoever has not witnessed, whilst abroad in society, the contemptible behaviour of a child left free to control its own mind and actions? It is akin to a *monster run riot*, unrestrained and unchecked, seeing fit to converse with whomever it chooses in a manner most hideous to behold! Who then has not looked upon the mother of this child with a mixture of pity and scorn? Such a neglectful mother is not fit to be welcomed into the arms of polite society; indeed allowing a child to behave so can only bring shame and disrepute upon a household!

With this in mind, we now endeavour to impress upon you the most crucial need to free your child of all his inner torments and to rid him of all his destructive character traits. In other words, you must *break your child's will* at the very earliest of opportunities and by any means at your disposal.

How to Break a Child's Will

Children are born inherently wicked and must be trained most vigorously to overcome the corruption within. A child is your property to treat how you will. It is to you, the mother, that the proper physical and moral training is committed, and it is you alone who has the opportunity to make the first most gentle and long-lasting impressions upon your child's nature. Does not a mother's influence mould and determine the very destiny of *all* society?

When first your child seeks to display a temper of prodigious volume and force (the usual age being between two and three years) and you have assured yourself he is suffering from neither illness nor pain, then you must begin at once to enlighten him in the error of his ways. A few stern words or a threatening gesture may be all that is needed; but rest assured that this is rarely the case. More often than not, you will have to resort to *corporal* admonitions which should be administered repeatedly until your child has ceased its dire display, or until he falls asleep exhausted. From this point onwards, your punishments should be repeated every time your child falters in his behaviour, until a mere glance or a single word is sufficient to haul him back onto the path of righteousness. In this manner you will succeed in breaking your child's will and be master of him entirely.

Many mothers favour the whip as a tool of correction as it delivers a swift and painful shock most effective in its consequences. The sting inflicted is likely to linger long in a child's memory and, if he should prove perverse, unable to learn spellings, or persistent in dirtying a frock, then a welt on the behind can only serve him well. For any mother not

fond of the whip, then a period of deprivation can be just as effective in breaking the will. Merely lock your errant child in his room for several days, nourishing him with only bread and water, and on emergence you will find his spirit most permanently and satisfactorily broken. This is a most useful treatment for those tiresome infants who are inclined to question your every instruction with 'Why?' They must learn that a mother need give no reason *why*, only that her will must be obeyed.

Those children who are very firm in their own little ways, that is, *wilfully* obstinate, will greatly benefit from a withdrawal of all your affections and a period of isolation. This method will spare a child many future hours of agitation and will cure in him any negative traits which may otherwise prove impossible to conquer. If this service should prove disagreeable to the young savage and he lashes out in protest, then a card worn on the back which reads, 'This is George, he kicks', or 'This is Georgina, she bites' will prove decidedly efficacious in bringing humiliation upon the disobedient wretch.

We have heard tell of devoted mothers of imagination, most wary of over-indulgence, who tie their wayward brats to the leg of a kitchen table for days on end – much to the consternation of the dear cook, no doubt!

We chance to insult your intelligence now by directing your maternal attention to the *injudicious* modes of corporal admonitions. A lash to the behind, to the back of the hand or to the back of the knees is most firmly recommended, but we would *never* advocate the same to be dealt across the head. The bones of a young skull are not yet firmly knit, and a blow to this area could render a child dull or indeed an idiot.

BASED ON THE HISTORY OF CHILDHOOD DISCIPLINE
IN VICTORIAN ENGLAND

How to Raise Self-Approbating Sons

'STEER YOUR COURSE SWIFTLY IN THE DIRECTION OF THE
CULTIVATION OF YOUR SONS' COURTEOUS GOOD MANNERS
AND SOUND GRASP OF THE APPROPRIATE.'

I t is the earnest wish of every young boy to grow to be
highly regarded. But by nature our sons are born petulant, impertinent and impulsive, incapable of pausing to
take into consideration the feelings of others about them.
Witness the reliability, for example, with which four out of
five of them will slam every door shut, without a thought
for the vulnerable nerves of their aged Aunt in the parlour.
Such sensitive attention to the needs of others must be
learned, if ever they are to better their natural tendencies
and elevate their characters to be worthy of society.

All our youth must come to a timely realisation that none
can be considered a gentleman who has not first been well
received by all who have made his acquaintance in boyhood.
It is apt, then, that we steer your course swiftly in the direction of the cultivation of your sons' courteous good manners
and sound grasp of the appropriate. It is the young man of a
self-approbating nature that can look to his *own conscience* to

seek confirmation of his good conduct in all matters; thus it is just such a young man whom you must strive to raise.

To this end, we will proceed to set out the essential guidance by which we should suffer our sons to be governed.

1. Beware above all else of the sin of idleness. It will bring about nothing but disaster: vices, crimes and misdemeanours all have their birth in an indolent character.

2. Do not permit your son to hamper his growing manliness in boyhood by adopting mannish vices: tobacco and alcohol, when consumed by a boy of twelve or thirteen, attack the vigour, health and conscience and weaken the resolve to excel in all things.

3. Do not tolerate a son who flits. If he is begun upon study, let him persevere with that for whatever length of time has previously been agreed upon. If he is absorbed in taking exercise or in play, let that too form the focus of his attention for an appropriate time. In this way will he cultivate an orderly mind.

4. Stamp out all tendencies to cheat. Fairness and justice in play foster fairness and justice in life. It follows that he must learn to abhor the lie and to seek to practise only the truth. Nothing else will suffice.

5. Forbid the indulgence of the temptation to stare. Insist that he adopt a countenance that appears to all the world as if he has not noticed the individual in question. No person, no matter how shabby, deformed or peculiar, must be spoken of by your son until well out of earshot. Anything else would be unseemly in a gentleman, and is no more acceptable in a boy.

6. See that he keeps good company. Though it may happen that a boy stumbles unintentionally into the company of one who proves bad, it is most commonly the case that he can deliberately opt for playfellows who are essentially good. It is a mother's duty to see that this is the case.

7. There can be no excuse for the mother who permits her son's rough treatment of the possessions of others. In almost every case, it is perceived as offensive for someone to show lack of respect for another's belongings in such a way. Courtesy and self-restraint in all things!

There is really nothing complex in the process of conducting oneself as a gentleman. Your aim, as a mother, is for your intervention to very soon grow irrelevant: with a little perseverance he will acquire that degree of self-approbation needed to carry himself as the perfect young gentleman.

❧

ADAPTED FROM ORIGINAL ADVICE IN WILLIAM A. ALCOTT'S *THE BOY'S GUIDE TO USEFULNESS*, 1844, AND OTHER NINETEENTH-CENTURY BOYS' ETIQUETTE MANUALS

How to Eradicate Worms, Lice and Other Infestations

'THE YOLK OF AN EGG BEATEN INTO A QUANTITY OF SPIRITS OF TURPENTINE WILL GENERALLY EXPEL THE WORM IF GIVEN TO A CHILD IN GREAT QUANTITY.'

Children are creatures of *natural* filthiness. Their disagreeable habits and dislike of clean water render them most attractive to all manner of vile parasitical beasts. It seems that a child cannot survive one month without being infested yet again with the worms or the lice.

There are numerous cures that will rid your child of these unpleasant visitors, but it is best by far that you rid your child of the *ghastly practices* that beget the infestations in the first instance.

Bid them not to fiddle with their ears or put their hands to their mouths, and to desist from blowing their noses with their fingers. Any child that is eating must not be scratching at any foul part. If it happens that they cannot help but scratch, then bid them to courteously take a part of their dress and scratch with that. It is better by far that the cloth be soiled than the fingers!

How to Eradicate Worms, Lice and Other Infestations

Lice: It is true that lice make an appearance only in the heads of those children who are unclean or bedridden by severe disease, so foster in your children a love of bathing that they may relish the sensations of a cold-water bath and benefit from its undoubted healthful effects.

Should it be that a child of yours is struck down with an illness which sees him long in bed, then have no doubt he will also be subjected to the merciless itchings of an army of lice. Take heed of the following receipts which are well proven in their efficaciousness against these most tenacious of all creatures.

Cut the hair short and wash the scalp most thoroughly with soap and water. Then apply a little benzene to the head, taking care to cover with a cap, so as to confine the suffocating vapours.

An ointment made from ten grains of white precipitate to half an ounce of lard and scented most strongly, may be smeared over the head for a day or two, much to the consternation of the vile parasites.

Part the hair here and there, and blow upon these places the smoke from a lighted pipe of tobacco. The lice will scurry to the outer reaches of the hair from whence they can be most easily picked out and crushed.

Bid your child to always carry a lavender-scented pomade to ward off re-infestation and to never associate with those of an unclean nature for whom the remedy is obvious.

Worms: The thread-worm makes its presence felt by producing a most intolerable itching at the fundament, by rendering the breath most disagreeable and by causing a child to grind its teeth and convulse during sleep. The following receipt is for one of the best remedies known and will frequently bring away a whole nest.

Digest in a bottle for one week, 2 ounces of liquorice, half an ounce of coriander seed, one ounce of socotrine aloes and a pint of gin. A teaspoonful given every morning is the correct dose for a child and the purgative effects will not be long in announcing themselves.

The tape-worm is a most troublesome creature, which can inhabit the whole of a child's internal canal. The yolk of an egg beaten into a quantity of spirits of turpentine will generally expel the worm if given to a child in great quantity. Failing that, pumpkin seeds taken copiously on an empty stomach will usually produce the desired effect. As a last resort, you may wish to pound together tobacco leaves and vinegar and place the mixture upon the stomach.

Proceed with caution, however, for tobacco leaves are especially dangerous to young children.

The Itch and Scald-head: These maladies are most infectious and we would urge you to keep your child at a great distance from beggars, farmers, travellers and those associated with the workhouses. If the infestations should take hold despite all best efforts, then make haste to employ the following receipts.

Baste a shoulder of mutton with tar and let it roast. Collect the drippings and rub well on to the scalp to rid a child of scald-head.

For the itch, beat flower of brimstone with common soap and add black pepper and hog's lard. Boil into an ointment and apply nightly by the fireside.

ADAPTED FROM ADVICE GIVEN IN *THE COUNTRY HOUSEWIFE'S FAMILY COMPANION* BY WILLIAM ELLIS, 1750

How to Care for Your Child's Skin

'URGE YOUR CHILDREN TO CONSUME A GOODLY QUANTITY
OF MEAT FAT: WHERE THIS CANNOT BE CARRIED OUT TO
A SATISFACTORY DEGREE, A DAILY DOSE OF COD-LIVER
OIL WILL ACT AS A GOOD SUBSTITUTE AND HAS A MOST
PLEASING EFFECT UPON THE COMPLEXION.'

All mothers blessed with any degree of sense will know that good skin is a mark of a sizeable measure of cleanliness. It follows therefore that a child or an adolescent exhibiting poor skin (and certainly those for whom the phrase 'poor skin' is most assuredly a *kindly understatement*) have descended into that sorry state as a result of a regime characterised by a most wanton disregard for basic personal hygiene. It goes without saying that the daily application of water to the skin is an essential. We would go further: to insist upon the careful employment of a good-quality soap. Not the caustic, yellow varieties, but the expensive, clear sorts, of which old brown Windsor is our personal favourite. Use the soap on faces daily, on the heads of children twice in every week and across the entire body at the very least once a week. For those who have the time, and are so inclined, one could do no better than to soap the entire body every day. This invigorates and unblocks the pores, keeping the skin at its most healthy.

The cultivation of *poor* skin extends further than simple hygiene. What goes into the body has as great a part to play upon the complexion as what is applied to its exterior. We heartily recommend that a child of five to nine years should begin their day with good bread and fresh milk at eight o'clock. At one, a hearty luncheon: roast mutton and apple pudding, or roast beef and currant pudding. Tea should follow at four: bread and butter, milk and water. Finally, supper at six: a light meal of bread and cheese or butter. Calamitous in the dietaries of adolescents are pastries, pies and cakes of any sort. As irresistible as they may be to a young palate, they stimulate the formation of additional red blood corpuscles, rather than the white sort that a nourishing diet will build up. Urge your children to consume a goodly quantity of meat fat: where this cannot be done to a satisfactory degree, a daily dose of cod-liver oil will act as a good substitute and has a most pleasing effect upon the complexion.

That certain grimy children may have been thus far neglected in the care of their skin, is inevitable, although unlikely to be a widespread problem in the better sorts of households. Nonetheless, we will devote a little attention now to the treatment of those disorders of the skin that are of a ghastly nature to behold.

Pimples

Pimples are a grisly abhorrence and firm action is necessary upon their very first appearance. Vigorous use of soap and water, followed by rough rubbing with a hard towel, is essential daily. In addition, five drops of dilute nitric acid and the inhalation (via a flue) of dilute hydrochloric acid, taken twice a day, will prove useful in most cases. Where this does not satisfactorily deal with stubborn pimples, as in potent cases of acne, arsenic may be required, in addition to the medicinal regime above.

Warts

Where warts appear in the form of a sizeable and regular crop, the only solution is a long course of arsenic treatment. A solitary wart is treated with caustics, though for those having the opportunity to travel, Sweden may be a good destination. There, the grasshopper *Gryllus verrucivorus,* identifiable by its green wings that are spotted brown, is highly sought after in the treatment of warts. This creature will bite off the wart and deposit a discharge upon its core that effectively eradicates it.

Blackheads

These appear as small black marks, commonly on the nose, chins and foreheads of adolescents. The application of a little pressure will result in a small white, worm-like matter being emitted. This startling substance is not, in fact, a worm at all, as is commonly thought, but a combination of fatty matter and dirt. Twice daily washing with good quality soap and hot water is the first course of treatment. After a three-week regime, the blackhead should be forced out from its gland by the application of two thumbs. Where this does not prove effective, hot flannels across the face for as long as can be borne, followed by the vigorous scrubbing of the area with a camelhair brush as a precursor to the above should be enough to secure a satisfactory result.

As a final word, those women who have most notably fine complexions (and these are always English women) are invariably found, upon further enquiry, to have daily used fine soap and a camelhair brush upon their skin since childhood.

❧

ADAPTED FROM ORIGINAL ADVICE IN CASSELL'S *HOUSEHOLD GUIDE*, C. 1880, AND HARRIET HUBBARD AYER'S *A COMPLETE AND AUTHENTIC TREATISE ON THE LAWS OF HEALTH AND BEAUTY*, 1899

How to Make Judicious Use
of the Cold Bath

'IF THE IMMERSION HAS BEEN SUDDENLY EXECUTED, TO
AN OPTIMUM DEGREE, HE WILL THEREAFTER BECOME
POSSESSED OF A PECULIAR CONDITION OF THE NERVOUS
SYSTEM, KNOWN AS A SHOCK.'

W e have a long inheritance of accepted wisdom when
it comes to the most healthful manner in which to
raise our young. Chief among this is the perception that to
plunge a youth daily into the cold-water bath is an immeas-
urably good thing. Alas, this sound inheritance is all too
often lost upon those we hire to raise our children; we have
all had the misfortune to encounter a nurse of such stubborn superstitions that no amount of urging will persuade
her to impart the medicinal benefits of this treatment upon
the children in her charge. Moreover, such dull-wits are
commonly insistent upon pursuing their own theories and
stratagems: such nonsense as dipping the child's clothing *a
set number of times* into water (for example, three or seven
or nine times), and thereafter suffering the child to wear

the sodden garments as they go about the business of the morning, or worse still, sending them to their beds in their dampened apparel. Others refuse to accept the virtues of any sort of bathing, putting their confidence only in water that has been dedicated to a particular saint. In such cases a mother may despair of ever succeeding in her entreaties to persuade the nurse otherwise, and her children will go without the cold water remedy for as long as she tolerates the continued employment of the wretched nurse.

But even in these cases, a good mother ought not to set aside the importance of the practice of immersing children daily in cold water. As a form of exercise, it cannot be surpassed and as a remedy, or tonic, it can prove invaluable. However, without due care and attention to the potential hazards of misuse or over-zealous cold bathing, there is undoubtedly much harm that can be done.

Rules of Cold Bathing

1 Ensure that the water is strictly at its natural temperature and has not undergone any degree of artificial febrile enhancement. The natural temperature will vary according to the season, and can be anywhere between thirty and sixty degrees.

2 Observe the natural stages of the phenomena produced upon the plunging of a boy of robust constitution:

   ❖ Firstly he will experience a sensation of extreme cold.
   ❖ This will be swiftly followed by an exhibition of shuddering.

❖ If the immersion has been suddenly executed, to an optimum degree, he will thereafter become possessed of a peculiar condition of the nervous system, known as a *shock*.

❖ Almost immediately on the heels of the shock will be a pleasant, warming sensation that will overcome his entire person.

❖ With this warmth still diffusing itself about his frame, he is to be *instantly* removed from the bath. (The timing of this removal is *vital* to his continued good health!)

❖ Now he must be thoroughly and vigorously dried with a rough towel, whereupon the combined action of the friction and the therapeutic water treatment will cause him to be thoroughly invigorated and be possessed of a vitality and an enjoyment of almost *animal* potency.

3 Reserve cold bathing for the summer; in the winter daily and vigorous ablutions of the entire body with a sponge soaked in cold water will adequately replace at least some of the tonic effects of the immersion treatment.

The Dangers of Over-Zealous Cold Bathing

The importance of removal of the boy before the sensation of warmth has been lost cannot be stressed highly enough. Allowed to become chilly once more, he will rapidly there-after grow also benumbed, which has an impact so injurious upon the child's physique that he will all too soon degen-erate into lethargy, fatigue and frailty.

Identifying the Child Who Would Most Benefit from Cold-Water Immersion

Look for the child who exhibits the following tendencies:

- ❖ Skin and flesh that is flabby and over-relaxed.
- ❖ A substantial inclination to warm perspirations in bed.
- ❖ A capricious appetite.
- ❖ Either oft confined, or else much relaxed bowels.
- ❖ A marked indisposition to exertion.
- ❖ Significant weariness from even the slightest effort.

In such cases, children will much benefit from daily immersion and may also require more radical measures: for example, relocating to a coastal position for a period of six months or more, and through the summer and winter, daily immersions in sea water, combined with a little controlled swimming therein.

ADAPTED FROM ORIGINAL ADVICE IN *THE MATERNAL MANAGEMENT OF CHILDREN* BY THOMAS BULL, MD, 1840

How to Protect Your Child from the Evils of Confectionery

'A CHILD ACCUSTOMED TO THE TASTE OF BOILED LOLLIES
WILL NOT BE LONG IN PROCURING FOR HIMSELF A FEW
PENNIES AND FINDING HIS OWN WAY TO THE SWEET-
MAKER'S LAIR.'

It is the *naturally* loving part of being a mother which
oft times fills a lady with the need to give pleasure to a
beloved child. It is not enough sometimes that the infant is
well-nourished, comfortably housed, warmly clothed and
suitably educated. Nay, a loving mother still feels drawn to
bestow upon a particularly charming child an *extra* token of
her love.

What lady of noble background, therefore, has not found
herself paying a visit to the confectioner's shop to fill her
pockets with all manner of penny candies, boiled lollies,
peppermints, lemon drops, sugared almonds and candied
fruits, with which to light up the countenance of her sweet
child? Who has not enquired of the comfit-maker what new
delights are on offer, and has then savoured the taste of an
exotic sugar flavoured with roses and violets? Have you then

not gone back to your home and witnessed the crunching of your offerings by the small teeth of your innocent child? Alas, you have been misguided in your kindness and it falls to us now to enlighten you in the error of your ways.

A moderate use of sugar at meal times we cannot strongly object to, there being no perceptible injury done, and likewise, the certain types of rock sugar purchased from the apothecary cannot be challenged, useful as they are for curing coughs, colds and stoppages of the breast. No, it is to the contents of the *confectionery shop* that we must draw your unwavering attention. The wares of these establishments can be considered nothing less than *poisonous,* especially those items that are frosted and coloured. Many have come near to losing their lives after gorging on a quantity of such temptations, indeed, we have it on good authority that extracts of chromium, and copper, mercury and arsenic are used to brighten the appeal of this produce of the devil. *The Lancet* itself has seen fit to declare these practices most dangerous! Even if one does not indulge in such a quantity as to fall sick at once, the smallest amounts of confectionery must slowly accomplish the work of ruination.

The infants and young persons who indulge in comfit eating, generally do so *between* meals. This produces mischief of the greatest kind. Not only does the stomach have to continue to work, when it should be at rest, but the appetite is completely ruined. Worse still is the dependence upon that feeling of excitement, brought on by simply *anticipating* the next lemon drop, that can result in a child becoming addicted to the sugar. We do not think you would wish any child of yours to become a fanatic. Think with

sorrow of those poor souls who live only that they may add sugar to their wine, make use of it as a snuff, and indeed, clean their teeth with a quantity!

But it is to the moral dangers of the confectionery shop that we must direct your greatest concerns. A child accustomed to the taste of boiled lollies will not be long in procuring for himself a few pennies and finding his own way to the sweet-maker's lair. It is here a child may happen upon the *very worst* of company – those debauched persons who find themselves addicted to all manner of excitements. Frequenting these palaces of pollution can only lead *directly* to the grog-shop, the gambling house, or (we blush at the mere mention) the brothel. An infant grown accustomed to the use of confectionery is but a short step from the road to gluttony, drunkenness and debauchery.

How to Protect Your Child from the Evils of Confectionery

We call upon all mothers of good sense and moral spirit: avoid at all cost the confectionery shop and never let a child of yours walk through the doors of that veritable chamber of death!

ADAPTED IN PART FROM A CHAPTER IN *THE YOUNG MOTHER, OR MANAGEMENT OF CHILDREN IN REGARD TO HEALTH* BY WILLIAM A. ALCOTT, 1836

How to Cleanse Your Offspring of the Sin of Self-Pollution

'THIS ODIOUS PRACTICE IS A PRELUDE TO NYMPHOMANIA AND, MOST DRAMATICALLY, HAS BEEN DOCUMENTED TO BRING ABOUT THE DISFIGURATION OF WOMEN'S PHYSICAL APPEARANCE, UNTIL THEY COME TO RESEMBLE MEN.'

The Original Sin of which we are all cleansed at Baptism is all too often replaced by another so heinous that it fills every God-fearing mother with fear and trepidation. Nothing is more self-polluting than the Secret Vice, that devil's snare in which so many of our youth can become entangled and at so tender an age. The medical consequences alone are frightful: drastic measures *must* be carried out the instant that the sin of Onan is uncovered. Should the practice be permitted to go unchecked, a young and impressionable mind would soon be overcome with such lasciviousness that, waking or sleeping, impure fancies would cause *involuntary defilement in the sleep*. Furthermore, the body can never be expected to recover until the habit is ceased, and a steady wasting towards mental and physical collapse can be anticipated.

In both sexes, self-pollution is known to affect adversely the nervous system, so that memory, understanding and paralytic disorders of all kinds will result. Indeed, at first signs of a dull, listless, pale and inactive demeanour in a child, a mother may be assured that she has in her midst one who is guilty of nocturnal self-abuse.

Syphilis, epilepsy, convulsions, dropsy, blindness and the most debilitating gouts are common consequences. In the male, Nature has deemed it necessary for good health that the seed be reabsorbed into the blood. Without this process, his masculinity cannot be reinforced from within, so that *effeminacies* are inevitable. In females, this odious practice is a prelude to nymphomania and, most dramatically, has been documented to bring about the *disfiguration of*

the women's physical appearance, until they come to resemble men. This process has been most infamously witnessed in the case of two Nuns of Rome, who finally changed sex completely, until they were wholly male. In addition, young ladies risk uterine haemorrhage, a falling of the womb, cancer, hysteria, emaciation, a haggard countenance and ultimately mania itself.

To this end, there are several steps we urge you to take. Firstly, see that you enforce a most rigid ethical and religious education. That God sees fit to punish this sinful disease with such fearful physical consequences, is proof indeed of the strength of His Holy Wrath in this matter. A mother must eliminate all sign of sloth: not only will this deadly sin breed uncleanliness, but furthermore, lust is known to stir in the bosom of the idle. Employ, too, a healthful degree of physical activity, such as would induce an easy and speedy slumber at night. Above all, impress upon your child the dire consequences of such an action. In both sexes, make it known that self-pollution will speed the wasting infirmities of old age.

Where such an abomination has not yet been identified, we would urge all respectable mothers to employ a thorough and trustworthy surveillance of their offspring, searching for signs of nocturnal pollutions. She may be assisted in her guard by one of several models of *protective devices*: garments that *encage the hazardous regions,* thereby preventing corruption. Especially noteworthy for mothers of sons troubled by amorous dreams is that device called the *Timely Warning,* a metallic brace that is strapped to your son's vulnerability and will prevent him falling victim to lurid danger whilst he sleeps. The metallic teeth of the instrument will take firm hold of any flesh held within, should it begin to expand or firm up, and the consequent pain will arouse him from his sinful slumber. Electrotherapy, most usefully used during a boy's sleep, has also proved most successful in eradicating somnolent sins.

Further reassurance may be sought in *surgical measures,* imposed widely upon the sons of the respectable and noble. These are most often resorted to in early infancy or in childhood, prior to sending a son away to school where so often he will fall victim to this obsession. This surgical procedure, wherein is removed that small section of flesh which is the most offensive, is furthermore a means to ensuring a cleanliness of body, as well as of spirit that, after all, combine to set him apart from the great unwashed.

Where a child has already self-polluted, a respectable physician must be engaged, who will be able to offer some assistance. For instance, the application of leeches to the appropriate area, or of acid washes, will be of much benefit in attaining a degree of cure. Whilst the body cannot ever be expected to make a full recovery, with medical support, and the grace of God, some good degree of health may be restored in time.

❧⟡☙

INSPIRED BY THE LATE VICTORIAN MASTURBATION-PHOBIA
AND BASED ON VARIOUS PUBLICATIONS FROM THE PERIOD

How to Breech a Boy

''TIS A SHAME INDEED TO FORCE A BOY SO YOUNG TO GIVE UP HIS PETTICOATS: HE IS SURE TO DO IT WITH ONLY RELUCTANCE AND REGRET.'

A doting mother, with all her natural feminine taste and tenderness, is disposed to *dread* the day she must breech her lovely young boy. From the very beginning she has relished in decking him in the finest of gewgaws and cosseting him in the most delicate of dresses. What proud mother has not looked upon her son, gambolling happily on the lawns in his white silk skirts and frothy petticoats, with collar of lace and the prettiest of ruffles? What adoring mother has not gazed with delight upon the shining ringlets bouncing upon his shoulders, curled to perfection each morning by the nursemaid?

It is indeed a delight to render one's son as pretty as one's daughter, to lavish on his costume the finest embroideries and lace that one can afford, and so useful to have a slender boy who can wear the discarded dresses of his elder sisters. A mother accomplished in the virtuous running of a household will be only too aware of the wise economy of this practice.

Many mothers will insist upon breeching a boy the very moment he is trained to relieve himself in the proper manner without need of napkins. But 'tis a shame indeed to force a boy so young to give up his petticoats: he is sure to do it with only reluctance and regret. There are too many delightful costumes of which to take advantage and so many fripperies in which to indulge, that the breeching of a boy may be most easily delayed till he is of at least eleven to twelve years of age. If an ungrateful son should wish to be breeched before you are ready to allow him, you may compromise by permitting him to wear a darling costume recently made most fashionable in Frances Hodgson Burnett's novel *Little Lord Fauntleroy*, with the dearest of plaid skirts and the whitest of collars and bow. We insist that you take a son so attired to a respected studio to have his portrait captured for all time, that you may forever remember his sweet innocence.

When the time comes, which it must invariably do, for you to make the momentous decision to breech your little man, we urge you to take all advice available. Do not come upon your resolution lightly, but consult with your husband, with the governess and with the nursemaid. Indeed, your son himself may have his own opinion on the matter, especially if he is of school age, when all his chums are already breeched and he has become the object of much teasing.

A glorious celebration must be organised to witness that first of breechings. Uncles and aunts and grandparents must be gathered together to honour the occasion that will present a new man to the world. Your son should first be brought down in all his luxurious glory, in the finest of dresses and with curls laid out lovingly to their best advantage. You may weep that the dress he wears would have lasted for a few further months and will now be wasted. Once admired and fondly petted he needs then to retire for the nursemaid to divest him of his wondrous ringlets. Your heart will ache when you see the soft carpet of curls spread o'er the nursery floor.

When next you see your son he will be an angel transformed into the dull and serviceable attire of a young gentleman. He will be stiff of gait, unaccustomed as he is to the confines of breeches and the cut of a suit. All will gather around him and line his virgin pockets with all manner of silver and sundries. The tailor will be called upon to provide a manly wardrobe and you may only hope that this loss of feminine attributes does not deprive your son of the very best of his characteristics.

BASED ON THE CENTURIES-OLD TRADITION OF
BREECHING A BOY

How to Send Your Son Away to Boarding School

'THEIR HEADS WILL BE SWIMMING IN NO TIME WITH THE
CONJUGATION OF VERBS AND THE ANATOMY OF A LANGUAGE
LONG SINCE DEAD. SUCH GROUNDING IS ENTIRELY
NECESSARY...'

There is no true gentleman of influence, moral fortitude or significant wealth that has not first received a
thorough education at either of the Oxford or Cambridge
Universities. For without that final seal, no gentleman can
be regarded as fully formed nor appropriately attired to
embark upon adulthood amongst this nation's political and
administrative elite. To this end we urge all mothers of
means to waste no time in signing their sons up for a place at
one of the seven prestigious educational institutions that are
the exclusive feeders of stock for those great universities:
these are Rugby, Eton, Harrow, Winchester, Westminster,
Charterhouse and Shrewsbury Public boarding schools.

The education your sons will receive once inside these
hallowed walls will be first rate. Thoroughly drenched in
the language of the Classics, their heads will be swimming

in no time with the conjugation of verbs and the anatomy of a language long since dead. Such grounding is entirely necessary: not for the development of their minds, nor to foster a manner of thinking that will be in any way of use or function in their daily lives as men. Far from it. Such languages are, by their very antiquity, utterly defunct and valueless in everyday society. But it is the fact that both Oxford and Cambridge insist upon a fluency in the Classics and, indeed, instruct in all subjects in that medium, that makes it so vital.

The question then is not *whether* a Mother should opt to send her son to boarding school, but more of deciding *at what point* such a move should be undertaken. This is largely a matter of taste and expediency. Some admirable mothers permit their little one to be sent off at the tender age of five years: certainly such an early start at developing that self-reliance so revered in a fine gentleman will give him an excellent advantage. Others are more emotionally inclined, finding it impossible to sever the apron strings until their son is as old as eight, still in ringlets and skirts! This will never do: a child will not toughen whilst it is burdened with such molly-coddling mothering.

Perhaps it will be of greater assistance if we try to elaborate a young boy's experiences of boarding school, by way of offering some enticement to the reticent mother?

If your son should begin his school days a delicate little flower, you may rest assured his transition into a tough young man, possessed of a brawny Christianity, will be speedy. The reputation of our great schools stands upon this: they offer an in-built, pupil-led rite of passage, known as the 'fagging system', by which they are able to turn out the calibre of young gentleman that has led this Empire to its current glory. Fagging introduces young students to the necessity of deferring to those of seniority and rank, namely the older students. Tasks are given out with relentless frequency and can range from the mundane, such as the cleaning of shoes, to the severe, such as the imposition of imaginative punitive measures. In this manner, generations of Officers are given their earliest training, albeit an unofficial one.

Your delicate flower will inevitably undergo a flogging on more than one occasion: fret not that this is an experience that is *at all* negative. For as long as he is spared, he cannot be considered a boy; moreover he will be derided and tormented as a girl by his fellow students. His first lash of the whip marks his first step towards manhood. Should your son at this point succeed in sending you sly word of his experience, shed not a tear, but leap for joy! For a good Christian boy can be no pacifist: how can he go on to lead King and Country into glory in the far corners of our Empire if he has not first survived an honest flogging or even a round or two of fisticuffs in the school quadrangle? We are sure that few will have failed to read of that infamous school-boy fight in the quadrangle of Eton in 1825, in which Lord Shaftesbury's brother was killed? Such losses are certainly tragic for a mother, but without one or two mishaps of this nature, Britannia would surely never have risen to rule the seas, as she most assuredly does today!

A mother must gird herself against the effeminising of

our nation's young men, and pack off her sons to boarding school at the earliest opportunity. The Empire depends upon it!

INSPIRED BY THE DEPICTION OF BOARDING SCHOOLS IN NINETEENTH-CENTURY LITERATURE

How to Deter Your Son from the Use of Slang and Coarse Obscenities

'FOREWARNED IS FOREARMED: POSSESSED OF A KNOWLEDGE OF OBSCENITY, YOU WILL THEREBY BE EQUIPPED TO ERADICATE IT FOREVER FROM YOUR HOME.'

The day will inevitably come when a dutiful and genteel mother must send her son off to school. He leaves her bosom the product of her unerring endeavours to raise a fine and well-mannered young man. He returns a product of that company he has there found. What transpires in the interim is often as if he has been taken overseas and his Mother Tongue translated into one so base, so alien and so repulsive as to make a mother wonder whether indeed this is her same son returned.

To this end, we have herein provided you with a list of the baser and more common terms of slang and coarse obscenities. It is our intention that forewarned is fore-armed: possessed of a knowledge of obscenity, you will thereby be equipped to eradicate it forever from your home, so that your son may emerge a gallant, well-spoken and well-mannered young gentleman.

Slang relating to Church & the Law

Autem-bawler	preacher/parson
Black box	a lawyer (also a *son of prattlement*)
Black coat	a parson (also a *soul-driver* or *spiritual flesh broker*)
A hum box	the pulpit

Slang relating to food, drink and clothing

Bever	afternoon luncheon
Bub	a drink (as in *rumbub,* by which is implied a very good drink)
Cackling-farts	eggs
Diddle	*Geneva*, a tipple favoured by the very lowest of people
Farting crackers	breeches
Flash	a peruke (as in *rum-flash,* referring to a long, much-prized wig; or *queer flash,* referring in turn to a sorry weather-beaten wig)
Gut-foundered	exceedingly hungry
Mish	shirt or smock
Queere-kicks	tattered old breeches
Rum-booze	wine or any good, strong drink
Stick flams	a pair of gloves

Slang relating to the body

Grinders	teeth
Gutter lane	the throat
Ogles	the eyes (as in *rum ogles,* meaning fine, bright, piercing eyes)

Pratts	the thighs or buttocks
Whirligigs	the testicles

Slang and insults relating to individuals

Back'd	dead (as in *he longs to have his father's back upon six men's shoulders;* or the taunt *his back's up*)
Ben	foolish fellow; a simpleton (also *benish* – foolish)
Bleeding cully	a fellow easily persuaded to fund all extravagancies of his mistress
Bob-tail	an impotent fellow, or a eunuch
Bottle head	one void of wit
Bracket face	ugly, ill-favoured
Fussocks	a fat, lazy woman
Fustiluggs	a fulsome, beastly, nasty woman
Hatchet faced	homely; hard-favoured
Jilt	a tricking woman
Sir Quibble Queere	a trifling, silly, shatter-brained fellow
Ralph Spooner	a fool

Other various terms

Baste	to beat
Bear-garden discourse	filthy, common, nasty talk
To filch	to cheat
Fogus	tobacco
Itch land	Scotland (also known as louse land)
Pike	to run away
Poisoned	big with child
Queere bung	an empty purse

To spunge	to drink at other's cost
Stubble it	hold your tongue

Coarse obscenities

In which we urge respectable mothers everywhere to desist from reading further – unless they have grim occasion so to do

Bauwdy baskets	pedlars who sell obscene books
Beard splitter	whore master (also known as a *brother of the gusset*)
Blower	a mistress or whore
Brother starling	one that lies always with the same woman
Bunting time	when the grass is high enough to hide young cavorting couples
Burnt	poxed or clapped (also *sun-burnt*)
Buttock	a whore
By-blow	one born to illegitimacy
Dandy prat	a puny fellow
To dock	to lie with a woman
Drab	a very nasty whore
Flap dragon	a pox or a clap
Gig'glers	wanton women
Hell-cat	a very lewd woman
Jockum cloy	to copulate with a woman (also *to jock* or *screw*)
Peppered off	soundly clap't or pox't
Thorough cough	the emission of wind through the seat whilst simultaneously coughing
Tip the velvet	to commit debauched acts upon a woman's privates by means of one's tongue

How to Deter Your Son from the Use of Slang and Coarse Obscenities

We most earnestly desire that none should find occasion upon which to refer to our dictionary. However, being ourselves mothers, we are not so blinded to the ways of young boys as to mistakenly believe that their innocence may never be tested by vulgarity. It is with this in mind, and with heavy hearts, that we have herein set out our brief dictionary of such terminology that needs be driven out from parlour, dining hall, parkland and schoolroom.

INSPIRED BY AND ADAPTED IN PART FROM *THE CANTING DICTIONARY*, 1736, AND *THE UNIVERSAL ETYMOLOGICAL ENGLISH DICTIONARY*, VOL. II, 1737, BOTH WRITTEN BY NATHAN BAILEY

How to Lace Up Your Daughter

'EVEN STRONG-WILLED YOUNG LADIES LEARN IT IS FUTILE
TO RESIST THE NECESSITY OF CORSETRY: THOSE WHO
PROTEST TOO LOUD AND LONG NEED ONLY BE LACED
TIGHTER.'

It is essential for any mother possessed of sound morals
to acknowledge when it is most prudent to strap a young
and impressionable daughter into a corset.

Many young ladies, upon reaching the age of twelve to
thirteen, are apt to show signs of boisterous and unladylike
behaviour, more akin to a rough schoolboy than a genteel
echo of their mother. Early introduction to the restraints of
tight lacing will not only banish unseemly conduct, but will
also encourage the youthful figure to grow in an upright
and elegant manner. Indeed, what mother would not wish
her daughter to be endowed with the tiniest of waists which
speak so eloquently of discipline, beauty and high culture?

A correctly fitted corset will, over time, bring about the
most pleasing of postures, correcting stoops and discour-
aging ungainly movements, idle lolling and gorging of
food.

It is wise to engage the services of a *recommended* corsetière to fit a daughter in the most appropriate manner. The finest of corsetières will advise in the very latest of scientific ideas and will endeavour to constrict a daughter in a way most suited to your needs.

Be mindful that any girl of tender years will be much opposed, at first, to the rigorous controlling of all her bodily movements. Do not be alarmed if she should swoon upon first being laced up. This is a most frequent occurrence amongst the youngest of ladies and, indeed, will become an alluring quality and one which she will call upon at propitious moments in the future, when seeking to attract the attentions of a desirable gentleman.

A newly corseted daughter should be informed in no uncertain terms that she is to bear any physical and mental discomforts with grace and acceptance. She will soon grow accustomed to her restrictions and will learn to appreciate and indeed revel in her proud and fashionable figure.

A daughter's first corset should be of a length sufficient to restrict bodily movement from her shoulders to her knees. It should be formed from heavy, rigid steels shaped into an S-curve at the rear to enforce an admirably arched back line. Her hips should be held well back and her bust held high. The corset should fit snugly when laced tight and should be constructed with at least ten steels or bones on either side to ensure maximum effectiveness.

For a daughter's comfort, a corset should be lined with a soft and supple kid leather. This quality material will prevent the corset from slipping round and thus save her tender skin from rubbings and chafings.

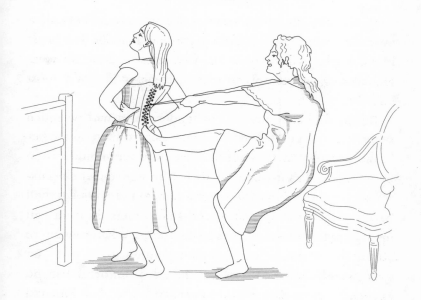

In order to hamper a daughter's effort to move independently of her corset, it should be solidly anchored both at the top and the bottom. Leather shoulder straps sewn tight to the top of the corset and buckled over the shoulders will prevent upward movement, and judicious use of corset boots will do the same down below. The boots themselves should be laced tightly to the leg and fitted with buckles to accommodate the leather straps sewn to the bottom of the corset. Straps both top and bottom should be adjusted to enforce a most ladylike carriage. Powdering and gentle padding may be required to prevent irritation of the armpits.

It is in the *constant* wearing of a corset that most benefits are to be found. Although a daughter may long for the solitude of her night-time chamber in order to escape from her confines, she will quickly learn that her corset is to be worn both day *and* night if a desirable result is to be achieved. Many a young lady may be tempted to loosen her laces whilst in the privacy of her bed, but a devoted mother will impress upon her the importance of *consistency* in order to attain the desired figure and to allow the internal organs to adapt. It is understandable that a young mind may give in to unbearable temptation when left alone at night, so it is your duty as a mother to prevent the ruination of all good efforts. Some soft padded cuffs fastened to a daughter's wrists and attached in a loose and comfortable manner to the bed, will frustrate any such night-time tampering.

The speed at which a growing girl turns from indulging in roguish horseplay to conducting herself with erect and graceful dignity will amaze and delight you. Even strong-willed young ladies learn that it is futile to resist the necessity of corsetry: those who protest too loud and long need only be laced *tighter* to be made to agree most readily with popular wisdom.

BASED ON AN ARTICLE IN *THE FAMILY DOCTOR AND PEOPLE'S MEDICAL ADVISOR*, 1889, AND OTHER ARTICLES ON THE HISTORY OF TIGHT LACING

How to Manage Your Daughter's Menstrual Flux

'ONCE A DAUGHTER HAS REACHED THE VERY BRINK OF PUBERTY, A MOTHER MUST BE RUTHLESS IN HER ACTIONS. HER DAUGHTER'S CONTINUED SANITY DEPENDS UPON IT!'

When her daughter reaches the age of fourteen or fifteen, it falls upon a mother to be alert to the signs that the girl will soon be visited by the tears of a disappointed uterus. She must educate her daughter well in advance of this momentous day, informing her of the natural sanguine discharge that she will imminently be subjected to. The dangers of concealment of such an event must be emphasised: much harm to the future health of her body and mind can result from a badly managed first menses.

We have heard tell from one A.W. Chase, MD, of the chilling transition that befell one poor wretch. Having been instructed by neither mother nor matron upon this subject, she took such fright at first sight of the staining of her clothes that she immediately went to a brook, where she washed herself and her skirts. This dangerous plunging of her person into cold waters, at such a time, instantly stopped her flow, which in turn set about a series of biological calamities within her person, such that she was rendered quite insane within a *matter of moments*. Think not that this tragedy is rare: our asylums are filled with hysterics, many of whom have fallen victim to their obstructed menses.

Once a daughter has reached the very brink of puberty, a mother must be ruthless in her actions. Her daughter's continued sanity depends upon it! To this end, we urge that a mother keep a tight influence over her daughter's diet, her emotional economy and the manner in which she spends her daylight hours. The diet should be heavily milk-based, with light, easily digestible meats and vegetables. At all costs avoid fruit, fish, tea and coffee. A girl should also avoid a languorous, indolent habit. Youth is the time of healthful frolics: never is it more important that plenty of exercise is taken than now. We urge mothers to see that their daughters indulge in gymnastic exercise: the jump rope, horseback riding, walking, running, the hoop and the game of battledore are all most useful in inviting the commencement of the flux. Flannel drawers, or other rough fabrics, are most useful too in providing some external pelvic friction that can tempt first menses.

All effort and watchfulness is essential on the part of the mother in order to ensure that the menses is thereafter regular and of an appropriate quality and quantity. (In respectable families, it may do well to have the head of the household, the husband and father, oversee this monitoring in order to make certain it is properly managed.) An obstinately delayed menses will wreak havoc, although the application of leeches to the vulva may help alleviate any immediate danger, whilst efforts are made to bring about the haemorrhage.

A young girl should be kept as cheerful as is possible during menses. Should she become possessed by any outbursts of fiery temper, caprices or intolerances of any sort they must be borne with resilience by all others in the household. To risk actively irritating such transient humours is to risk their radiation out from the uterus across the other organs of the body and, ultimately, to the brain. Warm baths, with infusions of balm and orange flowers, bed rest with the legs and thighs kept warm with bottles of warm water, should not be neglected as useful means of keeping good her flow.

During the haemorrhage she should refrain from washing at all in cold water; from any cold conditions; from iced or exciting drinks and from remaining outdoors without her arms and neck are covered. She should never sit upon a grassy bank or stone bench, for fear of close contact with damp. Vitally, all napkins used during the menses must be well aired and warmed in winter before use.

There has of late grown an increasing fashion for young women of keen wit to indulge a dangerous tendency towards learning. After puberty, this can only be disastrous for a young lady! We have had the misfortune of making the acquaintance of several ladies who have boasted high achievements in academic study. Botany and science are all very well, but all the bloods required by the brain in order to pursue such a course can only take away from the uterine flux, to a daughter's utter detriment. Mark you that all of these women of letters appeared unblessed about their bosoms (an affliction which cannot, in our humble opinion, be unrelated) and to our knowledge suffered a loss of that pelvic power that ought to be the natural state of women. Moreover, that same pelvic power *continued* to decrease in direct relation to the degree in which they persisted in the expenditure of their mental energies. Pelvic distortion, weakening of the womb, infertility and a tendency to hysteria will surely follow.

ADAPTED FROM ORIGINAL ADVICE GIVEN IN MARC COLOMBAT'S *TREATISE ON THE DISEASES AND SPECIAL HYGIENE OF FEMALES*, 1838, AND JAMES COMPTON BURNETT'S *DELICATE, BACKWARD, PUNY AND STUNTED CHILDREN*, 1895

How to Avoid the Bad Effects of Unwholesome Air upon Your Child

'NEVER ALLOW YOUR CHILD TO BE EXPOSED IN ANY WAY
TO THE COOLNESS OF THE NIGHT, 'TIS THE PATHWAY TO
FEVERS, QUINSY AND OTHER FATAL ILLNESSES.'

How many mothers, most fastidious by nature, have formed a proper regard toward the fatal effects of *unwholesome air* upon their infants? How many have unwittingly exposed an innocent babe to the dangers of a night-time breeze? How many have caused a child to suffer the stagnant draughts of a crowded church, with not one thought for the continuation of their good health? How many have set their child to sleep in the smallest of chambers, with shuttered windows and lighted candle, and found in the morning the child diminished in strength and health, or indeed that death had paid their little one a most solemn visit in the night?

It is our intention to apprise you of the ease with which the atmosphere is rendered impure and to bid you to grow accustomed to raising your children in only the most wholesome of fresh air.

How to Avoid the Bad Effects of Unwholesome Air upon Your Child

It is a little known fact that the perspiration is entirely obstructed by the night air and that evening dews are to be very much dreaded. Never allow your child to be exposed in any way to the coolness of the night, 'tis the pathway to fevers, quinsy and other fatal illnesses. Wherever there are great crowds of people gathered in one place, there too will the air be impure and noxious, there being no free flow of current. We have often witnessed the effects of this upon delicate persons in churches, who are apt to grow sick and swoon. It is no less harmful to a small child whose constitution has not yet grown robust. The atmosphere of great towns and cities is most abhorrent, filled as they are with the vapours of unclean bodies, the stench of slaughterhouses and the odours of horse dung. What manner of diseases lie lurking in these putrid exhalations, we shudder to imagine! It is of great importance therefore that you do not bring your child to the destructive air of the town, but let him remain in the freshness of the country until his education can no longer be avoided.

Many ladies of intelligence would imagine that a country estate would be the finest and most healthful place in which to raise a ruddy child. This may be so, but it is the *situation* of the estate that renders it either tolerable or unwholesome. Those houses which are surrounded by thick woods or which are situated close to great lakes or low marshes are to be avoided on account of the great quantities of *moist* exhalations that will abound and which dispose the body to fevers, dropsy and agues. We would bid you then to look closely at your estate and only be satisfied if it is built on a flat open space where the air flows free with little obstruction.

A child brought up in the correct manner is required to spend much of his time in the confines of the nursery. Much thought then should be given to the structure of this room and its daily ventilation. The nursery should be the largest room in the house and be situated on an upper floor to take advantage of the greater flow of air. It would be desirable indeed to have sliding doors that split the room in two so your child may retire to one half whilst the other is being ventilated. If it is not possible to construct your nursery in this manner, then you should bid your child get into bed and pull the covers over his head for the duration of the airing, should you wish to avoid him being exposed to the dampness of the air being introduced. A nursery must never be overcrowded with bodies; think of the perspirations, noxious exhalations and impure gases that two or three children and a nursemaid are wont to issue in the night and you will see how a build-up of these vapours can be most harmful to continued health. Indeed, a great escaping of bodily gases can poison a person outright if there is no chimney or any other place for it to disperse itself. We would advise you to sprinkle the floors and beds of the nursery with vinegar, lemon juice or camphor most abundantly and frequently to assist in the purifying of the air.

It is the business of the nursemaid to see to it that your children are taken into the open air for a sufficient period of time every day that the weather permits. A child will thrive most vigorously from this practice and will avoid the ghastly pallor so prevalent amongst those who have no regard whatsoever as to what may enter into their lungs.

ADAPTED FROM ORIGINAL ADVICE GIVEN IN *THE BOOK OF HOUSEHOLD MANAGEMENT* BY MRS ISABELLA BEETON, 1861

How to Instruct Your Child against the Over-use of the Direct Question

'A CHILD'S USE OF THE DIRECT QUESTION WILL SURELY BETRAY THE INCOMPETENCE OF THE PARENT AND CAST A SLUR UPON THE FAMILY NAME.'

The mark of true gentility may be found in the lilt of a beautiful conversation. Witness the art with which a gentleman leads a lady through an exchange, elegantly crafting an enquiry out of a comment and tripping effortlessly around agreeable topics and amusing matters of the day. Observe the lady as she *glissandos* between the phrases of a discourse, dainty and light-footed, her voice, laughter and vocabulary combining as a choir to sing her praises. In truth, to witness such a conversation is to witness a song and dance of such poise and grace that one believes oneself in the company of great artists.

Alas, this is not a talent which we are born with. It must be nurtured, instructed and rehearsed. And it falls upon mothers to carry out this tuition. Daily rehearsal of the rules of conversation set out below will soon pay dividends in all but the most hopeless of children.

The golden rule of conversation is to express an interest in your companion; to ask after them. But here is where most caution should be applied: instil in your child the *abhorrence* of the direct question! Such a coarse oratorical device is worthy only of the meanest street urchin, begging for its living, and should never be uttered from the lips of the genteel child. It is a contrivance considered by all of any import to be vulgar and boorish in the adult; in the child it surely betrays the incompetence of the parent and casts a slur upon the family name.

The practice must be stamped out in the nursery with a firm and consistent approach, before your children be ever permitted to sit in the parlour to receive callers. Equip them with appropriate alternatives: 'I trust that your journey was not made uncomfortable by the inclement weather' is infinitely more acceptable than 'Did you have a pleasant journey?' Furthermore, it is a more *precise statement*, and invites either a lengthy comment upon the event, or a brief response. In either case, it *demands nothing*. A son must be as well crafted in this as a daughter for, while in matters of business there may occasion a need for a direct reply to a direct question, in the world of society, he must become adept at dancing the merry dance of artful conversation with a lady, without ever committing the unforgivable *faux pas* of posing a direct question.

Where a child feels the need to seek assistance in a matter that cannot be resolved alone, he must be made to understand that in this instance it is *essential* he ask pertinently. For example, 'Would you be so kind as to assist me in this matter?' is permissible. 'Here, Mama, help me with this!' is not.

As to the other rules of conversation, they are obvious in nature to the well-practised; less so to the novice child. They should always smile pleasantly, in a manner that may not be misconstrued, as so many wilful or unguarded facial expressions may be. They should see that they are complimentary in their conversation, whilst avoiding flattery. Learning to appreciate the difference is essential. Where they are confronted with a companion who has not been blessed at birth by any natural grace of countenance, they should seek to compliment some other aspect they feel they may praise with legitimacy. (For instance, teach your child to see not so much the *portly* child with *abundant perspirant emissions*, but rather the *resplendent luminosity* that poor soul may be said to have about the face.) They should endeavour to be precise in their compliments about worldly things: they should never admire a fan, parasol or shawl, *per se*. Rather, they should single out a detail in the embroidery, colouring or fringing that warrants a specific mention. In these ways, a compliment will appear defensible, as it will have been grounded in specifics. An empty, unsupported 'compliment' is nothing more than worthless flattery.

They should avoid brash, dominant tones of voice. A daughter should strive to perfect that softly melodious timbre that is so becoming of a young lady. A son should seek to avoid any manner of conversation that will draw the focus of attention upon himself. Both should shun raucous laughter, as it is more befitting of a bar-room brawl than a parlour or dining room. Likewise, both should be drilled in the abhorrence of the interruption, the self-aggrandise-ment or the petty triviality. Their conversation should shine and sparkle, but not so brightly as to appear gaudy and distasteful.

ADAPTED FROM ORIGINAL ADVICE IN ASSORTED VICTORIAN ETIQUETTE MANUALS

How to Instil Filial Piety

'TEACH YOUR CHILDREN TO HONOUR YOU WITH THEIR
WORDS AND TO ADDRESS YOU WITH A TITLE OF RESPECT.
YOU ARE NOT A SERVANT TO BE IGNORED OR CURSED.'

There is nothing that will make you appear so respect-able and worthy in the eyes of others than having your children behave in the most dutiful of manners. Indeed, a child who honours *you* above all else will render you richer than if all the jewels and finery of the world were heaped at your feet.

It is an unfortunate fact that no child is born with an inherent goodness: they are blank slates, as yet un-chalked upon with observations of the world. It is your responsibility to lay the foundations of your child's character, and what more of an excellent and amiable character can there be, than one at whose heart lies filial piety? A young daughter who is respectful and willingly obedient is a most beautiful and charming sight to behold, whereas a daughter who is headstrong and self-willed appears as a monster, no matter how pretty her features. A son who submits to your authority with barely a whimper will reflect well upon *your* character, whereas one whose general behaviour is shoddy, will reflect dishonour upon you and allow others to say that your training and instruction leave much to be desired.

You must begin at once to make your children love you in such a way that they will obey you without question. From the earliest of moments you must impress upon your child that you expect nothing less than submission, reverence and respect. After all, will you not be sacrificing the greater part of your own life in rearing, supporting and educating each and every one of them? Will you not be sitting anxiously by their beds when they are sick? Will you not wear yourself out by caring so forcefully, and will you not render your husband old beyond his years by forcing him to labour long hours to provide for them?

With all that you are willing to sacrifice, should you expect anything less than to be honoured, respected and obeyed?

A mother who is truly honoured should never have to repeat the same command. Her instructions should be carried out most promptly and cheerfully. A child who answers back or indeed carries out the instruction with a sullen reluctance, a slam of a door or an ill-tempered stamp, must be made to endure the consequences of bringing grief and vexation to a mother's heart. It is by suffering a pinch, nip or a bob that a child grows quickly to see the error of its ways. You must impress upon your child repeatedly that by restraining him from hurtful and dishonourable practices, you are doing, what in the end, will benefit him greatly.

Teach your children to honour you with their words and to address you with a title of regard. You are not a servant to be ignored or cursed. Tell them that you expect no less than a respectful tone of voice at all times and to be addressed as Ma'am when in company, reserving the familiar title of Mother for only your most intimate of moments.

A child who does not always speak to you most politely, or one who may see fit to curse you under its breath, should be reminded of the pertinent verses in the Bible which state:

> *'He that curseth his Father or Mother shall surely be put to death.'*

> *'The eye that scorns obedience to his mother, the ravens of the valley will pick it out, and the young eagles will eat it.'*

That is not to say that we would *advocate* such courses of action, but merely hope that they would serve to remind a wayward child of the continued expectations of heartfelt filial piety.

INSPIRED BY THE HISTORY OF CHILD-REARING FROM THE 16TH TO THE 18TH CENTURY AND ADAPTED IN PART FROM *HOW TO BE A LADY: A BOOK FOR GIRLS, CONTAINING USEFUL HINTS ON THE FORMATION OF CHARACTER* BY HARVEY NEWCOMB, 1850

How to Train Your Daughter to Occupy Her Hands

'NOTHING CAN BE SO DISHEARTENING FOR A MOTHER THAN TO WITNESS HER DAUGHTER FOREVER RUFFLING HER SKIRTS, OR CONSTANTLY REACHING OUT TO STROKE FABRICS, BUTTONS OR THE TRIMMINGS OF SOME IRRESISTIBLE UPHOLSTERY.'

Every child requires training. If one faces a destiny devoid of the need to labour for one's living, one is *burdened*. For this predicament carries with it great responsibility and we must suffer our sons and daughters to acquire – and sustain – a spirited, self-reliant outlook at all times and in all things. Our daughters should strive for an open, easy manner; one which does not shy from revealing the tender hearts in their bosoms. They ought never to stem the flow of sunshine that pours out from their happy souls, drenching all they meet with warmth!

We are most often asked about the business of how a young lady should occupy her hands, that they may not meddle nor ramble about and thereby disappoint her gentility in all other respects. Nothing can be so disheartening for a mother than to witness her daughter forever ruffling her skirts, or constantly reaching out to stroke fabrics, buttons or the trimmings of some irresistible upholstery. This meandering hand is surely the mark of an untrained youth, but it is a sin of omission on the part of a mother if it is one that is not eradicated at the earliest possible opportunity.

Whether sitting, standing, walking or dancing, the hands must be a display of decorum in miniature. The fan or handkerchief is all too often the saviour of an ill-disciplined lady: having an accoutrement with which the hands may be occupied will suffice from time to time. But let it be a matter of principle that you cultivate the ability to sit, stand or dance with hands that are perfectly poised even when bereft of an accessory with which you may still them.

The art of dancing demands that the position of the hands is crucial: without elegant arms and hands, a dance becomes nothing more than elaborate stepping, after all. But to say as much, is not to underplay the degree of difficulty involved in perfecting the perfect carriage of the arms and hands, which demands a pupil's utmost attention and is by far one of the points of greatest difficulty in dancing.

Keep the arms in a graceful semi-oval position, with the bend in the elbow barely perceptible, when they are not otherwise employed in holding hands with a partner. They should rest a little in front of the body and only advance or recede in natural opposition to the feet, as in walking. The skirts are to be clasped gently between the thumb and forefingers of each hand, with the fingers grouped elegantly and held beautifully, with neither quiver nor rigidity.

It is easy to follow the argument that, if the hands are essential to gracious dancing, they also have a crucial role in the evident refinement displayed when involved in every other activity. Witness the lady who pays a morning call to an acquaintance. Her toilet is faultless in every respect. Her timing is impeccable and she pays homage to all those significant unspoken rules of etiquette pertinent to the parlour. But if, throughout her visit, her hands are constantly set to worrying her card case, or knotting and twisting her handkerchief around and about between her palms, she may rest assured that it will not have gone unnoticed and will certainly have been to the abhorrence of the lady of the house. Furthermore, her transgression will have been broadcast about within days – and rightly so! No lady of decorum can be readily forgiven for paying such a poor compliment to the lady of a house than to appear distracted, unfocused and impolite in the very extreme.

That is not to say that to carry a card case in one hand and handkerchief in the other is not entirely proper when calling. For it is true that these are the essential accessories of such an activity. But they must rest *entirely sedentary* in one's lap when sitting. And when occupied in walking, a lady who perfects the ability to hold her arms pressed lightly against her sides is justified in feeling that she has made no meagre achievement. This position will undoubtedly feel a little stiff at first, but perseverance will ensure that in no time it is graceful and natural and is surely the mark of a true lady.

ADAPTED FROM ORIGINAL ADVICE IN *THE YOUNG LADY'S BOOK: A MANUAL OF ELEGANT RECREATIONS, EXERCISES, AND PURSUITS*, 1829, AND *YOUTH'S EDUCATOR FOR HOME AND SOCIETY* BY MRS ANNA R. WHITE, 1896

How to Best Employ a Child

'EVERY CHILD, FROM THE EARLIEST POSSIBLE MOMENT,
MUST BE PRESENTED WITH A STRICT TIME-TABLE OF DAILY
EMPLOYMENTS TO INCLUDE RELIGIOUS TRAINING, TAKING OF
THE AIR, READING LESSONS AND NUMEROUS HOUSEHOLD
CHORES.'

A child is nothing more than a little adult and so should behave as one with all the accompanying responsibilities that are necessary to cope with the harsh realities of life. It is never too early to teach your child that there is simply no room in his day for misbehaviour, mischief or laziness.

The mind of a child should never be permitted to be idle for long; after all, is not a vacant head the devil's very own workshop? What pranks and roguery can be conjured up by irksome offspring left untended for too long and what measure of indolence can besiege a young body left to its own devices?

The young of all animals appear to be born with an innate fondness for amusement, and left unrestrained would indulge in this foppery to the point of fatigue. It is your duty to *impose restraints* and to concern yourself entirely with your child's moral disposition and his future place within society.

To this end, every child, from the earliest possible moment, must be presented with a strict time-table of daily employments to include religious training, taking of the air, reading lessons and numerous household chores.

Of chores most suitable for young daughters, none could be better than the sewing of repairs to petticoats and dresses. Indeed, all young misses by the age of four will be much practised in the art of needlework, able to stitch with delightful precision and neatness. The scraping out of stale wax from candlesticks and snuffers is a daily task young girls can excel at, building up an appreciation of household wastes and expenditures. They should be put to letter writing, caring for sick siblings and to the preparation of family meals, that they may learn the art of running a household and that their ladylike character may be suitably nurtured.

A young son may be gallantly employed about the estate. He may be set to feeding the animals and gathering firewood. He may learn to tame a wild horse and to shoot the game for his father's table. He must familiarise himself with every aspect of his father's business and conduct himself at all times as a young gentleman of good breeding.

If a child excels himself in his manners, duties and studies throughout the day you may permit him to participate in a suitable amusement of your *own choosing*. For a child to grow strong in mind and body it is necessary that you direct them at all times towards the *correct* amusement, a selection of which we now take the liberty of laying down before you.

The most healthful and fitting of all recommended

amusements is that of shuttlecock. It is suitable for both sons and daughters and you may be assured they will never tire of it. It is beneficial to the muscles, lending strength and power, and gives an accuracy to the hand and eye. It is the most perfect of pastimes, being decorous and none too robust. It can however prove injurious to the spine if played too frequently or for too long, so as in all things, you must dictate a degree of moderation.

A rocking horse is a most valuable addition to the nursery, arming a young rider with an essential love of horses and fostering an elegant poise and carriage. All manner of skills with the whip may be learnt whilst mounted upon this most faithful of steeds.

Young girls require a good deal of exercise and none could be better than the jump rope, which may be employed in the nursery on a wet day, or indeed outside on a fine day. A young man, however, would be better to be seen trundling a hoop or flying a kite, both of which employ a good proportion of the muscles of the body in such a manner as to greatly improve the health. We have heard it said that skating on frozen lakes in winter and swimming in rivers in summer are of hearty amusement to many young boys. They are not to be permitted, however, as they are activities over which a mother has no control.

Every young person, as soon as they are capable of a degree of comprehension, should be taught the agreeable game of backgammon. Not only is it highly amusing, but is continually instructive, exercising the brain in all manner of concepts and being of course most exhilarating to observe!

How to Best Employ a Child

It is essential that a thoughtful mother always sees fit to provide amusements that are healthy and instructive and *never* purely for delight. For, once a child seeks pleasure for pleasure's sake, therein lies the road to ruin.

INSPIRED BY A CHAPTER IN *THE YOUNG MOTHER, OR MANAGEMENT OF CHILDREN IN REGARD TO HEALTH* BY WILLIAM A. ALCOTT, 1836

How to Correct Skeletal Deformities with Dance

'WHAT USE IS A FINELY-HONED FEMALE MIND, WITHOUT THAT NECESSARY PHYSICAL DIGNITY WITH WHICH TO ATTRACT THE ATTENTIONS OF A SUITOR?'

꧁⁕꧂

How insidious is the destructive impact of the mother who insists that study and intellectual pursuits alone are necessary for her daughter's development and well-being? None can know this more readily than the great Dance Masters, as it is to these blessed individuals that the same mothers rush whenever they come to observe the physical devastation that such a course has inflicted upon their daughter's posture and poise.

A girl simply cannot be expected to sit hunched over her books or her writing for large portions of the day without dire consequences. During the act of writing, the entire spine is bent over to one side and the chest contracted. This will do nothing to ensure the graceful poise of the student and risks serious deformities of the spine if pursued for long. And what use is a finely-honed female mind without that necessary physical dignity with which to attract the attentions of a suitor? All too often this damage is merely extending the process of the gradual deterioration of her spine that was first brought on by her neglectful nurse. Too many nurses are wont to carry an infant about by gripping it firmly under one arm or other, which does untold damage to the alignment of the vertebrae of the spine and to the shoulder joints on that side.

Should you detect signs of just such a deterioration in your daughter, fear not. Simply seek out the assistance of a Dance Master of some local repute and be led by him in the necessary course of action. Take the case of Miss Emily Webster, of Chichester. So severe was the impact of her extended period of study that she was found to have developed a clearly detectable double curvature of the spine. Her mother, no doubt lamenting her woeful neglect, sought to remedy the situation by seeking out the immediate guidance of one of the region's finest Dance Masters. A regime of daily hour-long visits was prescribed. Within a month, sensible exercises and basic dance training was beginning to have remarkable effects: Emily's muscles were firmer, her wan hue replaced with a rosy countenance and her general health returned to something approaching robust. The exercises were increased to two hours' duration, then to three, until her graduation to perfect, straight-backed poise some months later!

Many of our most highly respected physicians have published treatises extolling the virtues of dance for strengthening weak and debilitated constitutions, for that repetition brings the muscles into beneficial action. Likewise, many of our greatest thinkers have remarked how early instruction in dance has the effect of raising the deportment, carriage and conversation of the child to that characteristic of one much older.

For those keen to make a start in this respect, there are some few exercises that you may instruct your daughters in at home, even without the guiding eye of the Dance Master to oversee you in your efforts.

Examine the fashion in which your child is wont to stand. Is she inclined to rest on one foot more than the other? If so, she risks the curvature of her waist to the one side and the raising of her opposite shoulder. This may be easily remedied. Insist that she stand as long as possible upon the opposite foot only. If necessary, have her hop about on it. Though she may resist, you may take comfort in her discomfort: it is evidence that this evil is being counter-acted with great effect.

The child who raises one shoulder too much must be made to carry a great weight upon its opposite, lower number. This will naturally cause her to raise it higher in order to support the burden.

A well-formed chest is essential to a graceful body: no lengths are to be spared in achieving your daughter's best advantage here. Have her grip her stays at her chest and sharply pull back her arms at shoulder height. This she should carry out with as much force as she is capable of, and should repeat for several minutes a day. Equally effective in this respect is the practice of having your daughter hold a stick at shoulder height and at arms' length for extended periods of time, without allowing her to drop her arms until she has reached her maximum capability.

How to Correct Skeletal Deformities with Dance

These small few measures may bring immediate ease to a mother's troubled mind, but cannot replace the daily instruction in deportment and dance from a celebrated Master. This is to be coupled with a stringent restriction in a daughter's study: in this path alone lies her skeletal well-being.

⋙⋘

ADAPTED FROM ORIGINAL ADVICE IN *BROOKES ON MODERN DANCING, CONTAINING A FULL DESCRIPTION OF ALL DANCES AS PRACTISED IN THE BALL ROOM AND AT PRIVATE PARTIES, TOGETHER WITH AN ESSAY ON ETIQUETTE* BY L. DE G. BROOKES, 1867

How to Manage an Hysterical Daughter

'IF A DAUGHTER SHOULD INDULGE IN FREQUENT BOUTS OF
LAUGHTER, CRYING OR EXHIBIT A VARYING DEGREE OF WILD
AND IRREGULAR BEHAVIOUR, THEN YOU CAN BE SURE SHE
IS GRIPPED BY AN HYSTERIC PASSION.'

The female character is one that is most delicately balanced, its natural state being that of a pure, pious and gentle serenity. With your good management, a daughter approaching the threshold of womanhood would hope to pass unscathed through her transition and so avoid the common and debilitating condition of hysteria that plagues so many of our kind.

When a daughter reaches the age of thirteen it becomes at once necessary to isolate her from all her young acquaintances and to have her in a place where you may exercise a continuous watch. It is well known that at this age the most violent of intimacies are formed between females that can wreak havoc with an innocent girl's most precious adornment – her modesty. It is as well to remove her from the source of these impressions and to prevent her, as much as you are able, from reading matter of a romantic nature or from becoming overly excited by frequent visits to the theatre. She must be made to abstain from stimulating drinks such as teas, sherbets and iced beverages and on no account should her feet be allowed to grow cold or her arms and legs be left uncovered. A daughter's thoughts should remain innocent until the day of her marriage, and to this end she must always be shrouded in a chemise while bathing and should keep her eyes closed when changing her toilet.

In this manner you may avoid the distress of hysteria which has brought many a young lady to the brink of insanity.

Being of honest persuasion, however, we would not seek to lead our readers into a false sense of assurance. All is never so straightforward in this world and, despite all efforts to adhere to the above advice, many outside influences may worm their way unseen into your daughter's organisation, unbalancing her character and unhinging her emotions. It is to this end that we lay down before you the means to identify an hysterical nature or an hysteric fit and the means by which to eradicate them.

If a daughter should complain of insomnia, faintness, a heaviness in the abdomen, a loss of appetite or if she exhibits a tendency to cause trouble, then you can be certain she is suffering from hysteria. The most immediate recourse would be to offer her up a variety of amusements, to lengthen her daily promenades and to place her amongst a cheerful company of your choosing. See to it that her diet consists of the lightest of animal food and an abundance of red wine. The cure consists of *whatever can strengthen* the whole habit and nothing will effect this more successfully than regular rides on a bicycle or on horseback.

If a daughter should indulge in frequent bouts of laughter, crying or exhibit a varying degree of wild and irregular behaviour, then you can be sure she is gripped by an hysteric passion. A compound of syrup of ginger, rust of iron and two drachms of galbanum fashioned into pills should be taken in quantity with a half glass of port until the passion subsides.

Once a daughter has been married off, you must not cease in your observations of her. It is well known that a wedded woman can succumb to hysteria to an even greater degree than a girl in puberty. You may find that, a few short months after her marriage, a daughter may slide into melancholy, spending her days languishing in her boudoir with nought but a dreamy look upon her countenance. Her behaviour may become unpredictable with scarcely a word or a morsel of food passing between her lips. This is surely hysteria at its most potent and must be treated as such. The family physician will be most skilled in the *pelvic massage*, a technique guaranteed to rid a woman of hysteria (if she sees to it that she attends his office on a weekly basis). His masterly administrations will eventually bring on an hysterical paroxysm which will at once restore the equilibrium and flush the cheeks.

We have heard of late that physicians' waiting rooms have swelled in number and many have grown weary of the tedious task of pelvic massage, with some patients taking hours to achieve hysterical paroxysm. It is with a glad heart then that we bring to your attention the invention of an electric home-massage device which can treat hysteria in the privacy of the boudoir. These devices are most readily available from every home appliance catalogue and promise to be 'very useful and satisfactory for home service'.

It may be as well to purchase such a device *before* a daughter weds and present it to her as a wedding gift, which will surely enhance her marital state and ward off the frustrations of hysteria.

INSPIRED BY THE HISTORY OF FEMALE HYSTERIA – A POPULAR DIAGNOSIS IN THE VICTORIAN ERA FOR A VARIETY OF FEMALE COMPLAINTS NOW BELIEVED TO HAVE BEEN A RESULT OF REPRESSION AND SEXUAL FRUSTRATION

How to Raise Your Daughter to Enjoy a Robust Constitution and Yet Excel at Needlepoint

'IT FALLS UPON US TO OFFER SOME SMALL GUIDANCE IN THE DELICATE MATTER OF ACHIEVING A DAUGHTER'S APPROPRIATE AND HEALTHFUL DEGREE OF EXERCISE, WHILST AVOIDING AN UGLY EXCESS... IT CANNOT BE CONSIDERED BENEFICIAL FOR A DAUGHTER TO EXERCISE TO THE VERY THRESHOLD OF HER FULL CAPABILITY.'

Far be it for us to attempt to counteract the faithful old adage that *actions speak louder than words*. For it is undeniably the case that a young gentleman will be the most captivated by the daughter who has been raised with a perfect feminine demeanour, so that she quietly shrinks from the slightest offensive discharge or rude blast. But a mother is *wholly mistaken* if she feels that achieving this goal of delicacy requires that a daughter shun *all manner of physical activity* in girlhood, whilst a son may roam about the countryside, developing that robust physique that will equip him for protective, assertive manhood.

Certainly, science instructs us that the body at birth is delivered ready equipped with a finite supply of energy and for a woman to utilise this unnaturally, with too much physical exertion (or indeed, too much intellectual exertion), can only diminish that supply needed for her mental balance and reproductive prowess. But to impose upon a female child a regime bereft of all physical activity, is to commit a sin of omission! For is not a daughter expected to grow to hover over the sick-bed; caress the eiderdown of the dying; and bear both the cantankerous irritation of old age and the petulance of youth? To begin her life with a marked want of exercise, then to be expected to live a womanhood of violent exertion, is a sure means to ill health, premature ageing and, moreover, to a pitiably poor wifedom.

Thus it falls upon us to offer some small guidance in the delicate matter of achieving your daughter's appropriate and healthful degree of exercise, whilst avoiding an ugly excess. There are naturally those activities which it would be not at all fitting for a young lady of refinement to indulge in. Swimming, for example, and competitive sports are so far removed from the boundaries of female decorum that it seems hardly worthy of warning. More suitable outdoor pursuits, for younger daughters, would be gentle gardening, brisk walks and, in the winter, sledging, skating and snowballing. On reaching the age of corsetry, walking, gardening and dancing are the most decorous exercise forms. Horse-riding too, naturally affords a young lady an entirely acceptable means of raising the heart beat and bringing a rosy hue to the countenance.

There is a great deal to be gained from *restricting* periods of outdoor activity. It cannot be considered beneficial for a daughter to exercise to the very threshold of her capability. Some period of time should be given over to a structured *indoor* regime that prepares her for the myriad other functions of genteel womanhood. For example, certain games are to be encouraged for your daughter and her female relations. Such games as foster social refinements are particularly useful. That of requiring participants to refrain from laughing or smiling, or else carry out a forfeit, is a means of gentle indoor entertainment that nevertheless affords a degree of useful training in the art of feminine restraint. The tossing of a decorative hoop from partner to partner by means of wooden rods, in the game commonly known as *Graces*, is particularly fine, requiring as it does, that each participant concentrates on moving with as much delicacy and grace as they can muster. This poise, whilst carrying out a task of some complexity, is excellent training for anything requiring a skilled co-ordination of the hand and eye (especially useful in the refinement of needlepoint and letter writing).

There can be no objection to the furthering of your daughter's intellectual capacity, so long as it does not stray beyond what is respectfully regarded as a *woman's sphere*. Cookery, for example, is a fine art and requires flair and skill to carry it off with that degree of aplomb that can lend advantage to any dining room wherein are assembled guests of great note. Musical skill at the pianoforte, a pleasant and melodious voice, fine needlepoint and a little light conversation in Italian are all most becoming in a young woman on the eve of her entry into society.

How to Raise Your Daughter to Enjoy a Robust Constitution

Add to this a degree of controlled, structured and feminine exercise and the result will be a daughter so robust, rounded, courteous, well-accomplished and fair of face, that she will not fail to swell your sense of pride in seeing your most important task so perfectly well carried out.

ADAPTED FROM ORIGINAL ADVICE IN EARLY NINETEENTH-CENTURY INSTRUCTION MANUALS, SUCH AS LOUISA C. TUTHILL'S *THE YOUNG LADY'S HOME*, 1847

How to Clean Carpets with Tea Leaves and Other Receipts for Keeping a Healthful Home

'A LOAF OF HOT WHITE BREAD SPLIT DOWN THE MIDDLE
SHOULD BE RUBBED EXTREMELY WELL OVER THE WHOLE
CARPET BEFORE IT IS SWEPT CLEAN WITH A BROOM.'

It is every mother's solemn duty to keep a home beautiful and sweetly wholesome. A constant and dedicated regard to all matters domestic will ensure that your offspring grow in refinement, intellect and moral sensibility. Indeed, the entire household will benefit from residing in a home where the bed linen is aired every morning; the carpets are swept daily, the furniture dusted, the sinks scalded and the cutlery polished to perfection.

The chief cause of a young mother's woe is that she has not been sufficiently schooled in these domestic duties, having spent much of her girlhood studying the delights of the pianoforte and the pleasures of the parlour. Do not despair; for it is not your path in life to be nursemaid, cook or housemaid. Indeed, these are the resorts of the lowest classes of women, *not* for those of culture and position. You need only to acquire some *knowledge* in the running of a household and be of sufficient temperament to instruct and control your servants in all matters. To this end, we take the liberty of laying down before you the most common of all household receipts that your domestics may flourish in their good habits and that your home may be forever unrivalled in its cleanliness.

How to Keep Carpets in Their First Bloom

A good and tasteful carpet will need to last a lifetime, it being one of the costliest items in your home. You must instruct your servants to lay crumb cloths in the dining room or in the parlour when the children are at play and to cover your carpet in the summer months with lengths of

canvas stretched and tacked down to protect the pattern from the ravages of the sun.

If there be any ink or grease stains then have them taken out with a lemon and afterwards rinsed with clean water. Then a loaf of hot white bread split down the middle should be rubbed extremely well over the whole carpet before it is swept clean with a broom.

It is useful to have your housemaid save all used tea leaves and to employ them, whilst still damp, in the lifting up of dust from the carpets. Simply have them sprinkled around, leave for a period of time and have them swept up along with the dust! You may find on occasion that the tea leaves stain the carpet. If this be the case you may prefer to use fresh cut grass which is just as efficient and lends a most pleasing brightness to your carpets.

To Remove Mildew from Linen

Have a quantity of soap and fine chalk rubbed well in to the mildewed linen which should then be laid out on the grass to dry. Repeating this process twice or thrice will remove the stains. Another method is to have brushed on to the doubtful linen a mixture of starch, soft soap, salt and the juice of a lemon. The linen should be left out on the grass for a few frosty nights to rid it of the stains.

To Remove Grease from Silk

Take a visiting card and separate it into two halves. Using the soft inner portion, rub it well upon the stain, which will disappear without taking the gleam off the silk. Another method is to mix together some fine French chalk with a quantity of lavender water until it resembles the consistency of mustard. This mixture should be laid on to the silk with a sheet of blotting and brown paper placed on top. The whole should then be smoothed with a warm iron.

For Cleaning Curtains and Sofas Covered with Worsted

Wheat bran rubbed on with a flannel is most efficacious in these matters.

On Cleaning the Parlour

See that all varnished furniture is only rubbed with silk and that all ornaments and books are dusted with feather brushes. When the parlour is to be swept, see to it that all the furniture is covered with old cottons.

How to Best Clean Steel Forks

A deep box filled with dampened sand and chopped straw is essential for cleaning blackened forks. Simply stab the implements several times into the sand, then use a hard brush to remove the grains from between the prongs and finally polish with an old glove.

INSPIRED BY *THE AMERICAN WOMAN'S HOME* BY CATHERINE BEECHER AND HARRIET BEECHER STOWE, 1869

How to Instruct Your Daughter in the Gentle Art of Letter Writing

'INSIST THAT SHE FOCUS ALL HER ATTENTIONS IN THE
LEGIBLE FORMATION OF HER CORRESPONDENCE ...
HER HASTINESS WILL RISK WASTING THE TIME OF HER
RECIPIENT, IF SPEED IS PREFERRED TO LEGIBILITY.'

When the duties of the household have been completed in full, there can be nothing more pleasant for a lady than to vary the hours spent at her needlework with a little letter writing. As with so much else of great value, a daughter is reliant on her mother to provide her with the wherewithal to perform satisfactorily in this gentle art.

Impress upon her the wonders of our post office! When she is requested to take into consideration all that passes through its hands in every week and, furthermore, how infrequently it occasions a mishap, how much greater will be her admiration for that marvel that is to be found in the writing, sending and taking delivery of a letter? In such a way will you easily create in her an earnest desire to perfect her art.

Firstly, see to her posture. All too often young girls

persist in their tendency to list to the left-hand side when engaged in writing at their desk, like some badly ballasted ship. Your first redress, should your daughter resist your spoken correction, is to suffer her to sit with her left elbow balancing upon a sturdy book (Culpeper's *Complete Herbal* fits the bill quite well in these cases). Alas, such is the folly of youth that very often this does not suffice and a mother's patience in these circumstances is tested quite to its limits. Your daughter simply will not heed your warnings. For not only are you conscious of her ungraceful silhouette, when her shoulders are imbalanced in such a hideous manner; you are also aware of the permanent *contortions to her shape* that can thereafter be resultant. But the wise words of the mature so often fall upon deaf young ears. If this is so, insist that she complete her letter writing with the *Complete Herbal* resting snugly upon her skull. In this way she will have no freedom to slouch to the left.

Next you must insist that she focus all her attentions on the legible formation of her correspondence. However hurried she may be to complete a letter and get it sent to the post office, her hastiness will risk wasting the time of her recipient if speed is preferred to legibility. This will never do. One may be the victim of correspondence of so poor a hand that one is forced to carry the letter about for several days, sometimes up to a week, and revert to studying and deciphering its coded hieroglyphs at every moment's leisure. Upon the completed translation one would be left most terribly taxed as if one had completed the translation of some tiresome Latin text. This ill-mannered imposition into another's time will never do. A young lady must pride herself in her perfect presentation in all things. Her correspondence must be no exception.

See that she details her address in full: nothing is more irksome than a writer who assumes you have retained their address from previous correspondence when this is blatantly not always going to be the case. Another quirk, peculiar to female letter writers, is the listing of the date as simply 'Thursday'. To name only the *day* in question is but a trifle; a tedious inconsequence, designed to portray the impression of some girlish silliness, no doubt. What good is a date that hasn't subsequently been grounded in a month and a year? Attention to detail, in all things, is the mark of a true lady.

So many ladies are given to another most wearisome of habits, that of turning a sheet through ninety degrees upon its completion, so as to resume writing upon the same sheet *at cross purposes*. Ladies, if your circumstances require that you impart some measure of frugality to your daughter's education, do so in all other respects but this! Desist from crossing a letter, if you value the continued sanity of your recipient at all! Upon reaching the end of a sheet of paper, we beg of you, take another. If needs be, you may take nothing more than a scrap. Pray, do not practise that absurd convention of cross-writing: it can do nothing better than to only elicit a *cross-humour* when it reaches its designated audience.

How to Instruct Your Daughter in the Gentle Art of Letter Writing

INSPIRED BY, AND IN PART ADAPTED FROM, *EIGHT OR NINE WISE WORDS ABOUT LETTER WRITING* BY CHARLES DODGSON (AKA LEWIS CARROLL) IN 1890

PS - Finally, may we highlight another much abused and over-used feminine *faux pas?* The *Post Script* is, for sure, an invaluable tradition, permitting the polite removal of some delicate matter from the *full heat* of the main body of the text and relocating it instead in the relative cool of the letter's dying embers. But it was never designed to be the siting of the main purpose of the letter, as is so often the case in the ineptly drawn up letters of certain frivolous and giddy-minded ladies. See that your daughter cultivates a direct, succinct and purposeful approach to her construction; impress upon her both the art of précis and the virtue of swiftly reaching the point. And leave the Post Script to fit the purpose for which it is intended!

How to Enjoy the Daily Hour with Your Children

'ONCE RESPLENDENT IN ALL YOUR FINERY AND GLOWING
FROM A DAY FILLED WITH USEFULNESS, IT IS NOW THAT YOU
MUST THINK TO SPARE THE MOST IMPORTANT OF ALL HOURS
TO LOOK UPON YOUR PRECIOUS CHILDREN.'

As mistress of the household it is your role to see to the comfort, happiness and continued social standing of your family. Your days will be filled with all manner of duties in which the feminine character excels. You must organise your time precisely, that you may benefit all with your intelligent and prudent attributes. We would declare it *requisite*, however, that you find time in your daily schedule to honour your *children* with your presence that they too may profit from your most essential qualities.

We herein take the liberty of laying down for your convenience, a recommended catalogue of daily requirements, listed in their proper order, that you may accomplish all that is required of you whilst releasing an hour of your day to enjoy in the company of your most splendid of achievements.

Begin your day at the earliest of hours. To rise promptly not only promotes a healthful constitution but ensures that your staff do not become sluggards. After all, have we not at times observed that a servant will take on some degree of their mistress's character?

See that your lady's maid has laid out a costume which is suited to the breakfast hour and any other domestic activities thereafter. Remember that your toilet must be adapted to your circumstances throughout the day, so the dress you wear at breakfast must differ from the one you wear to receive callers, to pay visits and to take the air. It hardly needs mentioning that full dress, with all jewellery and ornaments, must be assumed for dinner in the evening.

A fair portion of your morning will be taken with the checking of household accounts and the paying of various tradesmen. You need consult with the housekeeper as to the behaviour and industriousness of the servants and to the planning of the day's menu. After this general supervision, it is right that you give some time to the delights of literature, the heady pleasures of the garden and any estimable art in which you are possessed of talent, such as the pianoforte or the elegant pursuit of painting. It is pleasant then to visit the houses of the poor upon your estate where there will be many opportunities to instruct them in proper cleanliness, good industry and the art of cookery. Dispensing such valued advice will find you at ease with your conscience and quite ready for luncheon.

After enjoying a light but solid meal, you need prepare yourself for an afternoon of calls. There will be many courtesy visits to perform, most exquisite in their tedium, and you should limit your stay in each house to fifteen minutes only. Any longer would find you exhausted. You may also *receive* a number of callers yourself and should expect them to behave in the same considerate manner.

As the evening draws near 'twill be time for you to retire to your boudoir to rest a while and dress for dinner. Once resplendent in all your finery and glowing from a day filled with usefulness, it is now that you must think to spare the most important of all hours to look upon your precious children. Have the governess present them in the withdrawing room washed and neatened and possessed of their very best manners. There can then be nothing pleasanter than spending an hour in quiet and interesting recreation. Listening to a son read aloud a passage from the Bible,

hearing a daughter's practised composition on the piano and observing another daughter's delicate stitch to her sampler. What could be finer than witnessing this glorious testament to your mothering skills?

It is of incalculable value to your children that they know their place within the home, and for you to imbue them with this most respectful of characteristics is one of the choicest gifts a mother can bestow. When the hour is ended bid your children a most fond goodnight and have them returned to the nursery. Do not extend the hour for more than even a minute, it will fair overtax your emotions and render you too frail to excel at the evening's dining table.

ADAPTED IN PART FROM *THE BOOK OF HOUSEHOLD MANAGEMENT* BY MRS ISABELLA BEETON, 1861

How to Finish a Daughter

'IT IS REQUISITE THAT A DAUGHTER BE EXPOSED TO, AND DISCIPLINED IN, SUCH ELEGANT PURSUITS AS FLORISTRY, THE ESCRITOIRE, ENTOMOLOGY, RIDING, DANCING, PAINTING AND ARCHERY.'

A daughter is a precious object, of much use in the parlour and the boudoir and, one hopes, a gentle reflection of all that is much admired in her mother. During the latter period of her girlhood, when she stands on the threshold of the glories of society, much attention ought to be paid to the *finishing* of a daughter's finest qualities.

You must commence by building up your daughter's confidence, telling even the plainest of Janes how fair her face is. If you are persistent and fulsome in your proclamations then a certain aplomb will become evident in your daughter's demeanour which will do much to cover the inadequacies of Mother Nature's blessings. Instil in her a suitable love of costume that she may always present herself in the most impeccable fashion. Accustom her to the pleasures of society, that she may seize all invitations with much excitement and be discontent to *ever* stay at home. You must allow her to read nought but novels, and only those of a light and girlish nature; a young lady of *unusual* intelligence is likely to be spurned by every available gentlemen of *correct* society. Impress upon your daughter the notion that it is vulgar to be seen to be doing *anything for herself,* save those pursuits of an elegant and recreational nature: to this end, you may provide her with a lady's maid.

You would do well to send your daughter to a finishing establishment frequented by only *charming* young ladies, before launching her upon society. You can be assured that your good work will be honed and added to and that your daughter will be mixing in the company of girls unlikely to contaminate her young mind.

It is essential that a daughter's education be attended to at the *very best* of these establishments and that she is furnished with the accomplishments that will attract the highest order of husband. It is not necessary for her to be *mistress* of all skills, only that she acquires some *portion* of taste and assurance in these matters for, once married, these accomplishments become entirely superfluous. You need not concern yourself with educating your daughter in matters of an *academic* nature, it will not add one admirer to her list and will interfere with the delicate sensibility of her mind, rendering her quite worthless as a wife. You need only direct her towards those studies most pleasing to a potential husband.

It is therefore requisite that a daughter be exposed to and disciplined in such elegant pursuits as floristry, the escritoire, entomology, riding, dancing, painting and archery. (The latter is an unrivalled recreation, in which propriety permits a young lady to indulge. The practice of shooting at the target lends a general elegance to the carriage and the attitude of an accomplished female archer is most gratifying to behold.) It is to be hoped that your chosen establishment will ensure a course of escalated tight lacing to enhance deportment and would ration your daughter to prevent her growing unattractively rotund.

But, it is to the *moral deportment* of a daughter that most effort should be directed, for no accomplishment, however attractive, can compare to the virtues of character which must be instilled to render a young lady prepared for all the duties and trials of life. She must be furnished with a degree of goodness, purity and beneficence and be skilled at exhibiting all the correct sensibilities within the drawing room. She must be vigorously tutored in the art of swooning, able to faint away at the mere hint of a disagreeable topic or a scandal. She should be adept at the blush, pinking on the cheeks most deliciously whenever she is addressed and whenever she must reply.

If, after all of your most valiant efforts, you succeed in marrying your finished daughter off to a clerk or such upon £500 a year, then you may indeed congratulate yourself and look upon her situation as most fortunate.

INSPIRED BY A SATIRICAL CARTOON WHICH APPEARED IN
HARPER'S BAZAAR, 2 NOVEMBER 1867

How to Preserve Your Youthful Vigour

'IF WE OURSELVES LABOUR IN OUR ATTEMPTS AT AFFECTION
TOWARDS A DAUGHTER WHO IS DOWDY, A MOTHER WHO
IS GROWN BENT AND UGLY, OR A GRANDMOTHER WHO IS
OVERLY HAIRY ABOUT THE CHIN, HOW IN TURN MAY WE
EXPECT OUR MEN TO HARBOUR ANY OTHER RESPONSE TO
OUR OWN CARELESS COUNTENANCE?'

Any thinking lady must know and understand that youthful good looks and a vigorous constitution can only be the product of a twofold regime carried out by women of polite society. Firstly, these women will have adhered to a strictly *healthful* treatment of their internal faculties and workings. Secondly, they will have maintained a rigorous toilet, so that they are at the same time *externally* sound. The significance of maintaining a youthful appearance cannot be over-emphasised: women are unquestionably *better* if they keep their good looks, their youthful elasticity and girlish figures well into married life and motherhood.

Regrettably, it has been our experience that, all too often, marriage and motherhood plunge a once fine young lady into negligence and carelessness. She loses all personal charm, grows haggard, hairy and hunched. She either grows fat and bent, or wrinkled and emaciated even before she has reached what is, in the natural course of things, her prime of life. In this sorry state of affairs, the husband who hankered after the once breath-taking beauty he stood beside at the altar is correct in feeling that he has been robbed and cheated of the woman he married. Thereafter, without drastic action, the marriage, and the wife, are surely doomed.

With discipline and self-restraint, however, you may do your best to ensure that you give your husband no cause for complaint in the years to come. For are we not more enamoured of our *beautiful* daughters than of those who are plain? Is not our heart more inclined to love a *beautiful* mother or grandmother than an unpleasantly featured one? If we ourselves labour in our attempts at affection towards a daughter who is dowdy, a mother who is grown bent and ugly, or a grandmother who is overly hairy about the chin, how in turn may we expect our men to harbour any other response to our own careless countenance?

The medicinal marvel that is *Dr Hill's Tincture of Sage* is a vital addition to any lady's diet, the efficacy and potency of which has been well established throughout antiquity. A pleasant medicine, it will extend good health and youthful fine spirits even to the extremes of age. In warming the heart, preserving the mental faculty and strengthening the stomach, it will ensure that the rigours of motherhood do not sap you of your vitality. Upon imbibing it, one may feel instantly a gentle warming glow sweep across the entire body, the reviving heats of youth itself! A clear, alert mind and a jovial heart will be the next felt effects. At only three shillings a bottle, a teaspoonful daily in a wine-glass of water is all you need to bring about that restorative radiance. You will find it in Mr Baldwin's, the bookseller, in Pater-Noster Row, London, or else at Mr Ridley's, also a bookseller, in St James' Street, London.

Meanwhile, one must naturally adhere to a strict toilet that will work upon the preservation of youth *externally*. For this we may recommend nothing better than the advice of that genius of the feminine form, Mrs Harriet Hubbard Ayer, of New York. There, she has achieved renown for her patented facial cream, developed according to the highly prized recipe of a famous Parisian beauty, Madame Recamier, and thus sold under the name *Recamier Cream*. This wondrous ointment is guaranteed by Mrs Hubbard Ayer to remove all that redness and those other blemishes that are all too often the curse of the much over-exerted polite mother.

May we also urge you all to reject any decline into married dowdiness. There can be nothing more detrimental to the preservation of one's looks. Maintaining lustrous hair, a tidy and well-thought-out habit and scrupulously clean hands, face and body should be second nature to the debutante. To neglect this in spinsterhood is ill-advised; to do so within marriage is foolish; to do so within motherhood, thereby risking the continued happiness of husband and offspring, is nothing short of criminal!

Certainly there *are* features that are more challenging to overcome than others and often these can become more prominent with age. Freckles, for example, are not pretty and may grow stronger as years go by. But, in truth, they are *less visible* by gaslight: there can be no excuse for the freckled wife not to do her best in the evening, at the very least. Ravishing beauty may be out of reach for some, but there can be no cause for a descent into plainness. There is, after all, a respectable glory about feminine loveliness: no depraved woman ever was *truly lovely* on the eye; whilst on the contrary, there never was any moral danger in achieving and maintaining beauty.

INSPIRED BY AND ADAPTED IN PART FROM ORIGINAL ADVICE IN HARRIET HUBBARD AYER'S *A COMPLETE AND AUTHENTIC TREATISE ON THE LAWS OF HEALTH AND BEAUTY*, 1899

How to Work Outside the Home without Incurring the Wrath of Your Husband

'DO NOT HARBOUR ANY AMBITIONS TOWARDS SERIOUS
BUSINESS OR POLITICS, ESPECIALLY THAT WHICH REQUIRES
A CERTAIN DEGREE OF INTELLECT.'

There comes a time in every noble mother's life, when her domestic and maternal duties seem of trifling significance and she feels called upon to extend her refining influence over society by means of working *outside the home*. A woman who has long since seen her children progress from nursemaid to governess and whose household runs as efficiently as her servants' prowess, must surely grow tired of idleness. The endless afternoon teas lose their frisson, the pianoforte irritates the ear and the tapestry lies heavy in the lap. It is a great mistake, is it not, to limit the divine talents of a woman to the mere relations of marriage and motherhood?

But one must tread carefully, for there is the small matter of one's husband to consider. He that has long looked upon you as the Light of his Home and the Angel of his Hearth will not take kindly to losing your harmonious influence in the household, the effects of which soothe and cheer him during his evenings at home. He that has for so long been at the centre of your existence will surely react with nought but displeasure should you hazard to find employment elsewhere. That you should be rewarded in a pecuniary manner for such employment would surely render a husband speechless with indignation: it is his duty and *his alone* to provide for his family and his wife. Indeed, he would be brought to his knees in shame were it ever to become common knowledge that his spouse had contributed to the family coffers!

Being a lady of good breeding, however, you would never consider being rewarded for your labours with anything other than a sense of self-worth and a higher standing within society. Indeed, to earn *money* for your efforts would surely place you amongst the pitiful class of women who *sweat* for their daily bread. We therefore lay down before you our carefully considered words, which if heeded may find you gainfully employed outside the home with the full *blessing* of your dear husband.

Do not countenance industrial work of any sort; it is *entirely* unsuited to the female disposition. Likewise, do not harbour any ambitions towards serious business or politics, especially that which requires a certain degree of intellect. It is not appropriate either for you to aspire to running the estate while your husband is out of town.

No, it is towards *benevolent* work that you must direct your greatest energies and attention. What indeed could be more fulfilling than bringing tastefully arranged flowers to the sick and needy, or instructing the poor and dirty in the ways of cleanliness, or teaching the street urchins how to read? You may find your good works allow you entry into the most exclusive of male bastions; with a pounding heart may you find yourself reading Dickens to those incarcerated behind bars, and witness how they succumb to your maternal force!

To bestow your benevolence in this manner will surely enhance your name and good standing within society and serve to free you from the prison of your parlour.

You may wish to indulge yourself with scientific studies. It is most acceptable for you to take an interest in botany, natural history or ethnography. Indeed, you may elect to publish your findings in these subjects and gain a modicum of respect within your chosen field. Writing of any form, be it entirely whimsical or of a poetic nature, has become of

late most popular amongst ladies of a literary bent. Though it does not strictly take you outside the home, this occupation will render you *busy* and may gain you a certain repute. We have also heard tell that many ladies have taken to the studying of photography and indeed have become most competent in the art and in the handling of all equipment. There are also those who have become most efficient in the business of bird and animal stuffing, producing the most decorative objects to be displayed in the cabinets of all esteemed acquaintances.

Whatever your chosen occupation, be assured that your husband and children will be swollen with admiration for a wife and mother who renders such services to her community.

INSPIRED IN PART BY A LONDON WEEKLY NEWSPAPER, *THE LADIES: A JOURNAL OF THE COURT, FASHION AND SOCIETY*, FIRST PUBLISHED IN MARCH 1872

How to Battle with Barrenness

'BARRENNESS IS MOST OFTEN AN AFFLICTION VISITED UPON
THE AFFLUENT INDOLENT: THE LABOURING WOMAN IS
FAIR CURSED WITH EXCESSIVE FERTILITY, SO THAT SHE IS
CONSTANTLY TEEMING ABOUT WITH OFFSPRING.'

Of all the diseases peculiar to women, it is the unnatural shame of barrenness that is the greatest affliction for the rational woman. Without that sanctified satisfaction of the uterus in childbearing, the steady obstruction of the menses and subsequent degeneration into bodily and cerebral collapse is all but inevitable. It is for these poor souls that we herein offer some few words of advice.

It has come to our attention that barrenness has so often been the blight of women of general ill-health and weak constitution. It surely cannot be seen as a disease affecting any forced to work hard in life: the labouring woman is fair cursed with excessive fertility, so that she is constantly teeming about with offspring, whilst hatching yet more within her belly! For sure, barrenness is most often an affliction visited upon the affluent indolent, for it is these persons who have most probably indulged in high living.

Their languorous habits and rich diets are proved challenging in the extreme to their gut and digestions. Were they to model their lifestyles on those of the better sort of peasants about their estates they would no longer be forced to sit in envy of the copious product of the loins of their vassals. For indolence, that accursed habit of the well-heeled, creates a loosening of the solids stored within the body, as witnessed upon their expulsion. This is a sorry state of affairs, indeed, for one pining to procreate.

All is not lost, however, provided the lady in question is prepared to apply herself vigorously to the following regime:

- ❖ TAKE SUFFICIENT EXERCISE in good air, for there is nothing so detrimental to the body and mind as a deficiency of healthful quantities of good air. A lady should take as much exercise in the form of walking and horse riding as she can be expected to bear, certainly such as will foster an appetite for a good diet and restful sleep.
- ❖ SEE TO YOUR DIET. The significance of a milk and vegetable diet cannot be over-emphasised. Fish, meats, fruits, tea and coffee are laboursome to the digestion and cannot be seen as conducive to any fight against a barren, unproductive womb.
- ❖ ASTRINGENT MEDICINES will be of some assistance in this matter. Particularly steel, alum, elixir of vitriol or the Peruvian bark have all been noted as having achieved some success at undoing the curse of the barren.

❖ THE COLD BATH, above all else, is the true friend of the woman in need of procreation. Tunbridge waters in particular and the spa in general are also proved most efficacious in these matters.

Furthermore, we have it on good authority that the following receipt has enjoyed some success.

FEMALE STRENGTHENING SYRUP
Take of: comfrey root   4 oz
           elecampane root 2 oz
           hoarhound   1 oz

Boil them in three quarts of water down to three pints; strain and add while warm:

      beetroot pulverised ½ oz
      loaf sugar   1 lb
      brandy   1 pt

DOSE From half to two thirds of a wineglassful, three or four times a day.

Where barrenness has been visited upon one recently afflicted by grief, a startling fright or a great anxiety (passions that are wont to bring about an obstruction of the menstrual flux) it is in these circumstances understood to have been brought on by the troubled economies of the mind. In such cases as these all possible efforts must be made to secure the reinstatement of a cheerful and agreeable disposition without delay. To this end, a husband keen upon planting the seed of an heir must indulge his wife's every whim and entertain her every fancy; in short, he should make all manner of effort to amuse his wife. For it is only in the rebalance of the affections of the feminine brain that her uterine forces may once again be enabled to function as nature intended.

ADAPTED FROM ORIGINAL ADVICE IN WILLIAM BUCHAN'S
DOMESTIC MEDICINE, 2ND EDITION, 1785